PREACHING THROUGH THE CHRISTIAN YEAR 9

Sermon outlines for the Church seasons and other occasions

Robert Martineau

MOWBRAY
LONDON & OXFORD

By the same author:
Office and Work of a Priest
Office and Work of a Reader

Copyright © Robert Martineau 1983

ISBN 0 264 66939 8

First published 1983
by A. R. Mowbray & Co. Ltd
Saint Thomas House, Becket Street
Oxford, OX1 1SJ

Phototypeset by Cotswold Typesetting Ltd, Gloucester.
Printed in Great Britain by Biddles of Guildford Limited.

CONTENTS

NINTH SUNDAY BEFORE CHRISTMAS

A door open in heaven

> Revelation 4.1 (NEB) '*I looked, and there before my eyes was a door opened in heaven.*'
> Genesis 1.3 (RSV) '*And God said 'Let there be light', and there was light.*'

The tremendous truth which is enshrined in the story of Christmas, to which the Christian year begins to look forward today, is that God is not remote from this earth and unconcerned about it. Yet why should he be interested? This earth is a small satellite of a modest star in a very vast galaxy, which itself is only one of many millions. There was no need for God to have made this earth, let alone to have made us humans. The more one thinks about it the more wonderful and full of mystery the Christmas story is. If creation began when God said, 'Let there be light', Christmas is the occasion when Christ who is the light of the world was born. 'The light shineth in darkness, and the darkness comprehended it not.'

1 Between earth and heaven

The imagery of the Book of Revelation is not very different; 'there was a door opened in heaven'. Between earth and heaven, that is to say between man and God, there is not a closed barrier but an open door. Closed doors are the imagery either of rejection, keeping out the thief or robber who then tries to climb in some other way (John 10, 1), or else of captivity, keeping the prisoner in. Christ came, on the other hand, to 'open the kingdom of heaven to all believers'. He is the door, providing the way from earth to heaven.

1

2 Look for the door

We do not come to that open door as it were by chance. While one cannot press the imagery of the teaching of Jesus too far, he is not only the door but also the way. If we pass through life without a thought for Christ, spurning his invitation and ignoring his claims, we can scarcely expect to arrive at the open door. As the well-known hymn puts it, 'Christ is the path, and Christ the prize.' The Christian pilgrimage is a matter of travelling with Christ as well as to him.

3 God uses the door

Then again, it is clear that God wants us to find the door and pass through it. One of the secrets of the Christmas story is that the initiative is with God. It is God who seeks us rather than the other way round. If part of the appeal of the Old Testament is that we should seek the Lord while he may be found, the message of the New Testament is that the Lord came to seek us. As the hymn puts it, 'He came down to earth from heaven, who is God and Lord of all.' Yet while the infant Jesus was born once in time in Bethlehem, he can only be born again in our hearts if we open the door to him. Just as we cannot force our way to heaven by climbing in some other way than by the door, no more will Christ come into our hearts other than by our willing invitation.

4 An open invitation

We have also the assurance that we shall not be turned away when we reach the open door. 'Him that cometh to me, I will in no wise cast out' (John 6.37). There is an ancient story, apocryphal of course, which tells of the soul of Judas wandering in the darkness after his suicide. After a very long time in utter darkness, he saw a small light and moved towards it. As he approached it, he saw an open door and within was a supper table at which Jesus sat with the eleven disciples. It was the exact scene that he had left to betray his master. He heard the voice of Jesus calling to him, 'Come in, friend, we cannot finish without you.' There is indeed no limit to the love and mercy of God. We can humbly thank him, as Christmas approaches, that there is a door opened in heaven.

EIGHTH SUNDAY BEFORE CHRISTMAS

As in Adam all die

> 1 Corinthians 15.22 RSV (Post-Communion sentence ASB) '*As in Adam all die, so also in Christ shall all be made alive.*'

In these weeks which lead up to Christmas, we look forward to that great event in which Godhead and manhood came together. He came down to earth from heaven, who is God and Lord of all. The Word was God . . . and the Word was made flesh. The two natures were united in Christ. The Post-Communion sentence for today is a reminder of their great difference. Apart from Christ, we are very much 'of the earth, earthy.'

1 Man and God

In the first place, there is this gulf between man and God which is bridged by Jesus Christ. God is creator, and man is a creature. The adjectives we use to describe God, such as im-mortal, in-visible, are used to show that he does not share the limitations to which we are subject. We are confined to one place at a time, and are limited in all our ways; God is free and, being in-finite, can give all his attention to each of his creatures at the same time. We are subject to death, as our text reminds us; God is both immortal and the giver of life. At Christmas, that is to say in the coming of Christ, God shared all these limitations. Jesus was truly man, sharing our frailty, our restrictions and ultimately the death of the body.

2 Death and Life

Normally we would speak of life and death, because that is their order in our human experience. At a dangerous crossing in one German city, after World War 2, the American Army of Occupation put up a notice, 'Drive carefully. Death is permanent.' That is how most people feel about death; when it comes, that is the end. Apart from Christ, we have no grounds for thinking otherwise; nor can we escape death. In Adam, that is to say according to the flesh, all die. Jesus, in sharing our humanity, shared the death of the body. But as we know, his death was not a dead end; it led to the revealing of a life which death cannot touch. As he shared our mortal life, so he invites us to share his eternal life.

3 Nature and grace

The word 'grace' sums up so much of the Christian good news. Apart from Christ, before the Christmas event, we are 'under the law'. By nature we are grasping, impatient and selfish. In a sense we cannot help this, and so cannot be personally blamed for our natural state; a new-born infant wants food and cries if it is not satisfied. Nature says, 'Give me now.' Jesus Christ shared our nature. 'He was little, weak and helpless, tears and smiles like us He knew.'

But part of the secret of the Christian gospel is that our relationship with God is one of grace. By no amount of controlling the works of the flesh, that is to say by no amount of law-abiding behaviour, can we justify ourselves and earn our salvation. We are given our salvation through Christ, as an act of grace. He shared our nature that he might lead us into the realm of grace; and by grace we can enter into life.

SEVENTH SUNDAY BEFORE CHRISTMAS

Abraham's act of faith

> Hebrews 11.8 (Post–Communion sentences ASB) *'By faith Abraham obeyed the call of God, and set out not knowing where he was going, and came to the promised land.'*

It certainly calls for an act of faith to set out on a journey, not knowing where you are going; nor was Abraham's journey the kind of 'Mystery Trip' from which one is guaranteed a safe return by 7.30 p.m. Nowadays people like to have everything planned in advance; we want to know not only where we are and how we stand, but where we will be and how we shall stand, next week and next year. A diary two hundred years ago contained a detailed record of what its owner had done. A diary today contains a record of engagements in the future with forward planning notes for next year.

1 The element of uncertainty

It remains true, however, that even if we plan the future with the greatest care and in the greatest detail, there is always an element of uncertainty; even if we are more likely to see 'weather permitting' than 'God willing' on a notice about a garden fete. Long-term planning may depend on our financial stability, our health and that of our family and, for some plans, on the peace of the world. Some short-term plans may depend on freedom from breakdowns or punctures or accidents on the road. 'Some put their trust in chariots, and some in horses.' By way of contrast, the gambling industry trades not only on our acquisitive instinct, but also on the uncertainty factor which is so largely missing in modern life.

2 Faith as trust

Faith, as described in the letter to the Hebrews, is not a matter of belief in certain doctrines, but a trust which gives the courage necessary to face an unknown future. Faith may well be combined with hope, that is to say a confidence that the future is bright. On an earthly level, marriage is such an act of faith, The future may be unknown, but the parties to the marriage are more than ready to face it together, confident that joy lies ahead. 'Blind faith' is an unfortunate phrase. A blind man stands at the roadside, and a complete stranger comes up and offers to help him across the road; he puts his trust in the unknown stranger, as part of his faith in human nature.

This kind of faith is that which made the disciples answer the call of Jesus, 'Follow me.' They did not know where he would lead them, nor did he outline a programme like a leader of a political party. Any Confirmation candidate today knows far more about Jesus than the disciples did when they began to follow Jesus. They did not know where he would take them, but they were prepared to go with him.

3 Faith will be justified

Our text finally reminds us that Abraham's faith was justified; he came to the promised land. There are so many promises of Christ for us. There are the promises of strength (e.g. the bread of life), of Christ's abiding presence, and of a life with him which earthly death does not break. Just as the promises in the Old Testament about the coming of the

Messiah were fulfilled in the birth of Jesus, so our confidence is well grounded that Christ's promises to us will be fulfilled. Because we have this hope, we have good grounds to have faith in Christ not only in this life. (See 1 Cor. 15.19). Such faith involves a readiness to go through life with Christ, one day at a time. 'I do not ask to see the distant scene, one step enough for me.'

SIXTH SUNDAY BEFORE CHRISTMAS

Bread from heaven

John 6.58 JB (Post-Communion sentence ASB) '*This is the bread come down from heaven; anyone who eats this bread will live for ever.*'

1 Provision in the wilderness

In his Gospel, St John links the saying about the bread of life with the feeding of the five thousand, and that miracle with the provision of manna for the children of Israel in the wilderness after Moses had led them out of Egypt. Last week we were thinking about Abraham going out in faith, not knowing where he would be led. Under the leadership of Moses, the children of Israel knew where they hoped to go, even though they themselves did not know the promised land. Their journey, however, took them through an uninviting wilderness. The provision of food for such a journey was (literally) a superhuman task. What was provided was food for one day at a time; any that was kept (through greed and selfishness, or through lack of faith that God would provide the next day) was rotten and was not only useless but a handicap.

2 Provision for eternal life

In a few weeks we shall recall the message of the angels, 'Unto you is born this day . . . a Saviour.' Jesus came to effect a deliverance, which had many features similar to that associated with Moses, though it was from slavery to sin and the law and death rather than from bondage to an earthly overlord. As with the Hebrews under Moses, there is a long pilgrimage between the day of deliverance and the entry into the promised land. Jesus promised eternal life, life with him which is not broken by death, and promised it here and now while his followers were still in this world. Just as God provided bread for the journey to the children of Israel (and St John quotes Jesus as reminding his hearers that God did the providing, not Moses), so God will provide nourishment for eternal life during our pilgrimage. Jesus goes on to say that he himself will be our food: 'I am the bread of life.'

3 Provision for Christ's followers

Those who heard Jesus make that claim would either dismiss him as mad, or else would have realised that he was making divine claims. Looking back on the whole gospel record, we accept those claims; but it must have been much more difficult at the time. We can dimly grasp the fact that on the one hand Jesus gave his life for the world, so he gives himself to his followers. We associate that giving with the Holy Communion where, in a way beyond all human understanding, the life that was given for us is given to us. He came to share our life and make it possible for us to share his life. No one image is adequate to express such a deep truth, and this teaching of Jesus should be considered in conjunction with that of the vine and the branches. The branches of the vine share a common life, so long as they are united with the main stock of the plant; the life of the one flows into the other.

8

As with the manna in the wilderness, God gives us nourishment for the life of the spirit day by day. Each day God makes available enough strength for that day; we have to trust him that similar strength will be available tomorrow, and every day after. We are reminded of this in the Lord's Prayer, 'Give us this day our daily bread.' This thought is central in the teaching of Jesus, and does not only apply to daily bread, whether material or spiritual. It applies, for instance, to our thinking about and knowledge of God. We may think we know enough to justify our act of faith in trusting Jesus Christ to lead us to eternal life, but there is so much more to know and to experience. But then, this is all part of that sharing our life with Christ and letting his life flow into ours, which lies behind this image of Christ as the bread of life.

FIFTH SUNDAY BEFORE CHRISTMAS

Watch! 'tis your Lord's command

> Matthew 24.42 (NEB) '*Keep awake; for you do not know on what day your Lord is to come.*'

This text, of course, refers to the second coming of our Lord and has no original connection with Christmas. But leading up to the season of Advent, the message is clear and timely. Today's Collect, with its call on God to 'Stir up' the wills of his faithful people, reflects the same thought. The message is largely ignored today. We know when Christmas is coming on the one hand, and few people seem to be very concerned about the second coming. Some of our Lord's teaching about not knowing when burglars will break in is acknowledged as good earthly sense. We gladly take precautions and insure against as many earthly misfortunes as possible, but 'life's too short' to be worrying all the time.

1 Surprise meetings

The Gospels are full of stories of people who met Jesus once and once only; at least we have no further record of their having met our Lord again. In almost every instance the meeting was unexpected, though in some cases they had sought him out deliberately. The meeting with Zacchaeus is an example of the latter, though the meeting took a very different form from what he could have expected. The innkeeper at Bethlehem, on the other hand, was taken entirely by surprise though he could not have been expected to understand what had really happened in the stable behind the inn. Pilate and Herod had both heard much about Jesus, but in their judgement of him they judged themselves.

Indeed, in very many of the meetings recorded in the gospels there is an element either of an unexpected gift (such as healing) or of an unexpected crisis demanding a definite response. If the response of the disciples to the call, 'Follow me,' had been negative, we should never have heard of them again; the rich young ruler, we remember, found the demand too great. Yes, there is an element of judgement in meeting our Lord; that element of judgement is certainly enshrined in the thought of the second coming of our Lord.

2 Meetings bringing judgement

The element of the unexpected is very closely linked with the idea of judgement. In the parable of the sheep and the goats, which St Matthew places very shortly after the passage chosen as our text, the judgement is that when 'I was hungry, ye gave me no meat,' and so on. 'When saw we thee hungry?' is the immediate response. The opportunity and need for service had been there and had been missed. Maybe the opportunity had been taken, but grudgingly and for the wrong reason; what we really wanted to do was to get rid of what we thought was a scrounger. The opportunity for service is itself the occasion of judgement.

3 Meetings bringing blessing

Our unconscious meeting with Christ may also prove to be the occasion of blessing. Unless our eyes were open, we should very likely call it good luck or just a blessing in disguise. This again is the occasion of judgement. Nine out of the ten lepers who were healed did not turn back to say 'Thank you,' even though they knew the source of their healing.

Keep awake is the keynote of this season. Be on the alert for opportunities of service, for in serving others we are serving Christ. Be awake, and thankful, for the blessings which Christ brings to us.

> Watch! 'tis your Lord's command,
> And while we speak, he's near;
> Mark the first signal of his hand,
> And ready all appear.

ADVENT 1

The blind seeing

Isaiah 35.5 (AV) '*Then the eyes of the blind shall be opened.*'

Not to be able to see God's good world is indeed a distress which should call forth the sympathy of all right-minded

11

people, and the care of the blind should receive their help and support. Some doctors accept it as their vocation in life to devote their skill to give sight to the blind, not only in this country but in the Third World where blindness is more widespread. Those of us who do not have that skill can support organizations (such as the Royal Commonwealth Society for the Blind, and the Guide Dogs for the Blind) which do their work on our behalf.

1 Gratitude for seeing

At the time when Isaiah wrote his prophecy, it was commonly believed that blindness was the consequence of sin, a penalty (almost a curse) inflicted by God. We get a glimpse of this in St John's Gospel when he tells of the healing of the man who was born blind; the Jews asked Jesus, 'Who did sin, this man or his father, that he was born blind?' You remember the answer of Jesus that it was neither, but an opportunity for the love of God to be shown. Indeed, the Jews who were standing by had to make up their minds whether the healing of that blind man was an act of God or not; if it was not, was it one evil casting out another? In fact, of course, all healing is the work of God. The doctors and nurses are doing God's work, they are God's agents; we are right to pray for them, and to 'give thanks for the operation of their hands'. Those of us who can see should thank God often for the gift of sight.

2 What do we see?

But how do we use our eyes? What do we look at, and what do we see when we look? There are some who, having the gift of sight, use it largely for the satisfaction of their lower senses. The books they read, the entertainment they watch, the sights in which they delight, are a shame even to think upon. What they see with the outward eye becomes imprinted on their

12

mind and helps to form their character. What a travesty of the use of sight. Better were it for some, maybe, if they had been born blind (cf. Mark 9.47). There are others who have to witness sights of evil, which they would far rather avoid; such has been the lot of many for whom close contact with evil and pain has not brought contempt. By the power and grace of God the spirit of sympathy has been awakened, and a sensitiveness to suffering aroused, which before was dormant.

3 Seeing and perceiving

Our eyes are a window of our soul, and our minds act as a filter. It is a big step from seeing to perceiving. How much of the teaching of Jesus starts with the things that can be seen, and leads on to what can be perceived. The care of God for the birds and the generosity of the widow with two mites are but two examples out of many. Sir Arthur Eddington at the Observatory at Cambridge used to say, 'I do not understand how anyone can look at the stars through that telescope, night after night, without believing in God.' Sight is given that we might have perception. It follows that true beauty should adorn places dedicated to the worship of God so that, by the vision of the outward eye, the heart may be uplifted; and not only places of worship, but our homes and neighbourhood should speak to us and to others of the beauty of the God of creation.

In one ancient (Syrian) manuscript of the Gospels there is an interesting variant reading. The two blind men at Jericho are asked by Jesus what they want him to do for them; they reply, 'Lord, that we may see *thee*.' (Matt. 20.33). That is indeed the hope of every Christian, the gift of Christ to those who trust in him.

ADVENT 2

The deaf hearing

Isaiah 35.5 (RSV) '. . . *and the ears of the deaf unstopped.*'

We thought last Sunday of the gift of sight and how the
coming of Christ opened men's eyes to see the Light of the
World. Isaiah goes on to say how the coming of the Messiah
would open men's ears to the word of God.

1 Gratitude for hearing

As with sight, let us start at the earthly level. Do we thank
God for the gift of hearing? Quite apart from the radio or
television, or going to concerts (or even Church Services)
hearing is one of the chief factors in making possible the
fellowship of home and association with friends. Fortunately,
as with blindness also, the medical and social care of the deaf has
advanced greatly in recent years, but it remains a severe
handicap for many. This has not prevented some deaf people
from holding positions of influence in Church and State.

2 What do we hear?

But there are two kinds of people who are deaf—those who
cannot hear and those who will not listen. A lot is done for the
first group, and the Church has an active ministry to the deaf;
but little can be done for those who will not listen. Perhaps we
should ask ourselves what we listen to most readily, and, of
what we hear, what stays in the mind and memory. (You
remember the man with whom everything went in at one ear
and out at the other, like water on a duck's back!). But
seriously, what do we allow to stay? If we listen to unkind

14

gossip, to cheap slander, or to dirty jokes, does it stay to poison our outlook?

There are plenty of biblical references to people with itching ears, including the men of Athens to whom St Paul preached on Mars Hill (Acts 17.21). In the explanation of the parable of the sower, our Lord speaks of several kinds of hearers; some just hear the words and pass on to other things, some are intrigued for a while and then distracted, some have not enough depth to let what is heard have its effect, and a few hear and understand, are enriched and fruitful (Mark 4.14–20).

3 God should be heard

When speaking of hearing, Isaiah presupposes a God who speaks and mankind who should listen. Indeed it is remarkable how often the imagery of speaking is used of God, from the Genesis record of creation, 'and God said,' onward. By the word of the Lord were the heavens made. The prophets believed themselves to be used as the mouthpiece of God: 'Thus saith the Lord.' God speaks the word of command, the word of warning and the word of encouragement, the word of judgement and the word of love. He conveys these words to men in a whole variety of ways. Nature is full of cautionary tales, and so is the past history of man. In every age there have been prophets, used by God to speak his word. Some have not been aware of the fact at the time. Has that never happened to you when someone has said something which struck a deep note (of conscience, or encouragement), but who could not have realized the effect of his words?

On this Sunday in particular, we think of the Bible as the word of God, one of the chief ways in which God speaks to us. Its authority is accepted by the Church as decisive; but it needs to be pondered and understood. Clearly it contains all kinds of literature—history, poems, words of caution, promises and so on. When we have read a passage, we must ask ourselves, 'What is God trying to say to me through this?' Sometimes it is

15

obvious, at other times it is much less so. If prayer is conversation or intercourse with God, we must listen to him and not do all the talking. In other words, Bible-reading should go with prayer just as much as prayer should go with Bible-reading.

But Isaiah speaks of the effects of the coming of the Messiah; the ears of the deaf shall be unstopped. If the word of God has been spoken through the prophets, how much more through Christ, as our readings at Communion on Christmas Day will remind us. (Heb. 1 and John 1). Yes, God has spoken and still speaks; he that hath ears to hear, let him hear.

ADVENT 3

The lame leaping

Isaiah 35.6 (AV) '*Then shall the lame men leap as an hart.*'

This means so much more than that the lame man will be able to walk again. Leaping implies joy and gaiety. The same word is used in the Acts of the Apostles, where Peter and John heal the lame man who sat begging at the gate of the temple (Acts 3.1–11). It is used figuratively by Elizabeth at the visit of Mary: 'the babe leaped in my womb for joy'. This prophecy of Isaiah is not just speaking of healing the lame, but giving them a joy which is out of this world.

1 Leaping implies freedom

Walking and leaping imply freedom and release, but it may take time. When the concentration camps at Dachau and Buchenwald were relieved, there was, I am told, an almost unbelieving hushed response; the inmates took a long time to

16

react to freedom. Restriction and limitation wear down the soul as well as the body. Indeed, though it did not apply in those cases, familiarity with restriction can breed a satisfaction with one's own condition so that one does not want to get better. This is implied in the question our Lord puts to the man at the Pool of Bethesda, 'Do you want to be made whole?' (John 5.6). We can, as it were, 'enjoy bad health'; and this can apply to our souls as well as our bodies. Our moral weakness becomes so much part of ourselves that we not only do not believe we can be cured of them, but do not want to be.

2 Freedom from the bondage of the law

One aspect of the freedom which Jesus came to bring is described by St Paul as freedom from the bondage of the law. This is not to imply that morality does not apply to the Christian but rather that he is controlled by the spirit of Christ instead of by the letter of the law. One speaks figuratively of being tied down by a mass of regulations, and this did apply to the strict Jew; indeed it still applies to the strict Jew today. In a sense, we are all controlled by a mass of rules and regulations. It is equally easy to let our religion become a matter of keeping rules; we may call them pious habits, but in reality they are rules. Our church-going practice and, maybe, even our times of private prayer and Bible-reading can become a matter of rule – a restriction on our freedom rather than an expression of it.

3 Freedom for joy

It is difficult to draw a dividing line between freedom (which is not licence) and law (which is not bondage). But one decisive factor is the element of joy. The coming of Christ brought joy to the world as the Christmas carol puts it; and this joy is meant to be with us all through the year, and not just at Christmas. Equally, this element of joy is not always evident in the lives of the most habitual worshippers. Yet a gloomy Christian is really a contradiction in terms – in the same way as a selfish Christian, or an unforgiving Christian. Of course there are moments when things get us down. But whatever trials we have to face, Christ has faced more and conquered. Real Christian life is not so much a matter of following the example of Christ, as of living in the strength of Christ.

Christmas brings a time of joy and gaiety into an otherwise dull season; letting Christ into our lives can do the same. This prophecy of Isaiah still holds good. At the coming of Christ 'the lame man shall leap as an hart'.

ADVENT 4

The dumb singing

> Isaiah 35.6 (RV) '. . . and the tongue of the dumb shall sing.'

1 The joy of singing

Christmas and singing certainly go together. Christmas hymns and carols are both the best-known and the most popular of all. People who come to church on Christmas Day (next Sunday) would be bitterly disappointed if they did not have a good sing. Singing expresses one's feelings, whether the sad lament, the sentimental song of love or the outburst of joy. Singing is the most common imagery in the Bible for the activity of heaven and symbolizes not only the expression of joy and adoration, but also the harmony (and peaceful co-operation) of those who are involved. Indeed our singing of praise at Christmas is an echo of the angelic chorus, 'Glory to God in the highest and on earth peace, goodwill towards men.'

2 The duty of singing

As with the other parts of this prophecy, Isaiah is thinking of those who either do not or cannot express themselves in this way. If they cannot, then indeed they call for our sympathy and for all possible medical and social help; this is all the more important, since blindness or lameness are obvious handicaps but dumbness can easily be misinterpreted as mental backwardness. A great deal of hurt and offence can be given by such an attitude. But quite apart from those who are physically dumb, there are many who do not use their voice. They may not be 'mute of malice;' they are just silent. Perhaps in a sense they are similar to the blind or the deaf. Where there is beauty or majesty or evidence of goodness and love, they just pass by without comment. Even if they notice these things, they are not stirred to thanks or praise; they just take everything for granted. Week by week goes by without their joining with the Christian family in worship; day by day goes by without a word of thanks for the continued blessings of God.

> New every morning is the love
> Our waking and uprising prove;
> Through sleep and darkness safely brought,
> Restored to life and power and thought.

Sooner or later, silence from praise and thanksgiving breeds a condition of ingratitude, gloom and despondency. (This can apply to a group, a church or a nation, as well as to individuals). It takes something from outside to happen, to change things.

3 The incentive for singing

This is where the prophecy of Isaiah is so important. The coming of the Christ is just such action on God's part, enough to stir us out of monotony into a joyful outburst of praise. In a sense, the meaning of the word 'gospel,' or good news, is that what God has done has given us something to talk about. But while our neighbours and workmates don't want us to be preaching at them all day, do they have grounds to know about the faith that is in us? If we were keen supporters of Nuclear Disarmament, or Women's Lib., or one of the political parties, our colleagues would soon know. Are we among the dumb, to whom this prophecy applies? At least at Christmas time we shall sing; sing for joy, let yourselves go.

CHRISTMAS

Mary kept all these things

Luke 2.19 (RSV) '*Mary kept all these things, pondering them in her heart.*'

When the first Christmas was over, maybe the innkeeper and some of his guests remembered that a baby had been born in the shed at the back. 'Poor girl, having her baby just when the census was on. I hope they're all right.' The shepherds would remember, of course, and the wise men from the East. But Mary kept all these things, pondering them in her heart. And when Christmas is over for us, what shall we remember most?

1 Secrecy and significance

The secret meaning of Christmas was hidden then, and is largely missed even now. Indeed we make such an event of the season that the message is not easily heard. The song of the angels is drowned by the noise of men.

And man, at war with man, hears not
The love-song which they bring;
O hush the noise, ye men of strife
And hear the angels sing.

Two men were walking down the Mall, with all the traffic going past. 'Stop; did you hear that?' one of them said, 'Fancy hearing a linnet in a place like this.' It may not be entirely true, but it is largely so, that we hear what we listen to. The same applies to the things we see. Lots of people, besides the Wise Men, must have seen the star of Bethlehem. Even if it had been bright, most people would do little more than say, 'The stars are bright tonight, aren't they?'

Whether we like it or not, we tend to associate important events with either noise or light, or both. The ambulance, police-car or fire-engine announces its presence with a siren and flashing light – quite rightly – and the siren has to be loud enough to be heard above the din of the traffic. Advertisements flash on and off to attract (or distract) our attention. Yet is probably remains true that the most important events in people's lives are those which are least well-known to the world at large. It is certainly true in the life of a parson; the most significant moments in his ministry are those about which he never speaks, and about which only one other person, in each case, knows anything. In much the same way, the importance and the secrecy of Christmas go together.

2 The secrecy of our souls

War is noisy, peace is quiet. Contrast the quiet of Christmas (*Stille Nacht* – Still the night) with the violence of the murder of the infants by Herod's soldiers. Yet the latter doubtless received some publicity. By all means let us celebrate the birthday of Jesus with much thanksgiving each year. But the event that took place so unobtrusively nearly two thousand years ago is mirrored again and again, equally quietly, in the hearts of men.

> No ear may hear his coming;
> But in this world of sin,
> Where meek souls will receive him, still
> The dear Christ enters in.

21

Christ wants to be born again, in our hearts. To change the illustration, he stands at the door and knocks; it is a gentle knocking, not a loud battering. When we let him in, he and we are the only ones who know about it at the time; others may notice the change in us later, but they will never fully understand the difference it has made to us.

3 Secret nurture

Mary understood Christmas in a way that no one else could, but it was not all over when the babe was born. She now had to care for him, nurse him and bring him up to mature manhood. While she 'pondered these things in her heart' she could not spend all her time looking back. And it is the same with us when Christ is born again in our hearts. We cannot spend our time reminding ourselves (and others) that on such and such an occasion we let Christ come into our lives. A lot of silent after-care is needed. Perhaps as we receive the outward sign of the bread and wine, in assurance that we wish to receive in our hearts (by faith, with thanksgiving) the very life of Christ himself, the truth of Christmas is being repeated. Its meaning will be remembered by us long after all the outward festivities are forgotten.

SUNDAY AFTER CHRISTMAS: NEW YEAR'S DAY

This is the year

Psalm 118.24 (AV) '*This is the day which the Lord hath made; we will rejoice and be glad in it.*'

New Year's Day is a Sunday this year. Our first act (apart from domestic preliminaries) is an act of worship. We might adapt

22

the text from the Psalms, 'This is the year which the Lord hath made . . .' This is Anno Domini 1984 – the year of our Lord; it is his year, and we are invited in. It is like a corridor with 366 rooms, at each of which we knock and hear the Lord's voice, 'Come in.' All our years, all our days, are lent to us. Let the first act of each week and the first act of each day be an echo of what we are doing now.

1 Look backward and forward

At the turn of a year, one can look back and forward. Look back with penitence and with thanksgiving. Even the penitence can be coupled with thanksgiving, for God loves us and accepts us just as we are, in spite of what we have done or become as a result. To that extent we can leave the past behind. Obviously some of the consequences of our actions will have to be carried forward. If you broke your leg yesterday, it will not be mended by today; nor will your bank wipe out your overdraft. But each new day and each new year is a gift from God, a chance to start afresh. Looking forward in hope and in trust, we can say, 'So long thy power hath led me, sure it still will lead me on.' Christ will go through the year with us; we need not be anxious. 'Though I walk through the valley of the shadow of death, I will fear no evil; for thou art with me.' Even if George Orwell were right, God will see us through!

2 Carry on the normal

Some of the hymns specially written for early mornings have some strange verses. By all means 'Awake, my soul, and with the sun thy daily stage of duty run,' but must we 'Live this day as if thy last'? It depends on whether the prospect of a day being our last worries us. John Wesley was once asked what he would do tomorrow if he knew it were to be his last day on earth. He replied that after his time of morning prayer, he would try to fulfil all the engagements planned in his diary and in the evening, as was his custom, he would ask God to accept and use all that he had tried to do for him. In other words, he would carry on as normal.

3 Be thankful

What are we going to do about New Year resolutions? Or are you so disillusioned with past failures that you have given up the idea? It was (I think) Charles Simeon, the great evangelical preacher, who looked at the end of a year at the list of resolutions made at its beginning. Almost all were broken. One was kept: 'each day this year I will thank God for something different, without repeating myself'. As a result he was a much more thankful man, and his eyes were more open to the goodness of God.

> When all they mercies, O my God,
> My rising soul surveys,
> Transported with the view, I'm lost
> In wonder, love, and praise.

Perhaps we might be wise to start in a small way and do it for a week, and then later for a month.

4 Be confident

As we look ahead into the coming year, we do not know what lies ahead. Like the Wise Men, led by a star, we do not know where we shall end up. But God does know. He has prepared for us 'good works for us to walk in': a happy phrase. Wherever our path leads us, there will be opportunities of service. He has also 'prepared for them that love him such good things as pass man's understanding'. Travel with Christ, and you can look ahead with confidence.

Bethlehem of noblest cities

Matthew 2.8 *'Herod sent the wise men to Bethlehem.'*

It was very understandable that the wise men should have gone to Jerusalem, if they were looking for a newly-born king of the Jews. It was, after all, the capital city and the centre of rule and authority. Rather obviously they were asking the way, and they were given the right answers when told to go to Bethlehem. What seems a little strange at first sight is that, if the scribes and teachers of the law were really expecting the Messiah to come, they might have been less taken by surprise. They were quite definite with their answer: the Messiah would come out of Bethlehem, the home-town of the family of David, where Ruth had settled many generations before.

1 Lowly Bethlehem

The ancient prophecies were indeed fulfilled, but the revelation was given to some outsiders; those who ought to have known were unaware of what God was doing. Bethlehem was a very small place and apart from its connection with the origins of the family of David (but what a large exception) had little other claim to fame. Evidently the prophecy of Micah (5.2) was poetic praise, and a harking back to the past. Times had changed since then.

2 What Christ gave Bethlehem

Both St Matthew's Gospel and the letters of St Paul stress the fact that in Jesus the prophecies of the past were fulfilled. The Jewish people believed they were chosen by God to be the guardians of his law, not just for themselves but for all men. St Matthew constantly uses the phrase, 'that it might be fulfilled which was spoken of the Lord by the prophet. . . .' The old covenant was now complete and the new covenant established. In this sense, Bethlehem belonged to the past; yet the birth of Jesus made of it something new and gave it a glory exceeding anything it had before. What applied to the place, Bethlehem, applied also to the Jewish people. Our thinking about them and our estimate of their importance among other nations is coloured by the fact that most of our knowledge comes from the Old Testament. But they were not a powerful nation, and at the time of Christ were under Roman occupation. The birth of Jesus revealed their past significance and at the same time gave them a unique place in the history of mankind.

3 What Bethlehem gives us

What the birth of Jesus has done for Bethlehem his birth in our hearts can do for us. However suddenly it may appear to happen to a few people, it has always been the will of God. Indeed it is the will of God that all men should be saved. (1 Tim. 2.4). There is long preparation by God through the course of events for our readiness to welcome and receive him. When a Confirmation candidate stands up and says, 'I turn to Christ,' there has been long preparation not just by the vicar. The influence of parents in a Christian home, and the influence of their parents on them, is but a part of that preparation. School, society, friends and church are other means used by God to help to make the decision come about. In other words, the decision has firm roots in the past. Equally it transforms our life for the future. The transformation is so great that Jesus describes it as being born again, (John 3.3), and St Paul says that we become a new creature (2 Cor. 5.17).

Finally, just in case we glamorize Bethlehem after the birth of Jesus, perhaps we should remember those young mothers who mourned the loss of their infant children murdered by

Herod's soldiers. Obviously this was the sin of man, not the will of God. Maybe that is another story, but it can act as a warning against being too soft and sentimental about the Christmas story.

EPIPHANY 2

Insignificant Nazareth

> John 1.46 (NEB) *'Nazareth!' Nathanael exclaimed; 'can anything good come from Nazareth?'*

It sounds as though it were a common proverb that nothing good came from Nazareth, perhaps equivalent to the feeling that anything with the label 'Made in X' is shabby. Nazareth was in Galilee and there was a saying that no prophet would come from Galilee (see John 7.52), but it sounds as though Nathanael's remark is a general expression of scorn. Nazareth, where Joseph and Mary had their home (and where Jesus would have been born had it not been for the census), was a town of no great importance; it is not mentioned in the Old Testament. It was not evil, just insignificant.

1 Prejudice

Unfortunately, Nathanael's remark is echoed only too often today, not about Nazareth but about countries, races and classes. Colour prejudice is very deep-seated, not just in Southern Africa, as inner-city rioting in recent years has shown. Religious intolerance is also very deep-seated, not only in Liverpool and Northern Ireland. Anti-Semitism was not a temporary feeling, confined to Germany at the time of Hitler. The attitude, 'Give a dog a bad name and hang him,' is all too common and all too unconscious. In time of war and conflict, these feelings are whipped up. Because the leader of another country has led his people into conflict, we condemn all the people of that land; we have seen this reflected in the field of sport in recent years. Perhaps Nathanael's remark was more significant than he realized.

2 Christ breaks through divisions

Obviously as man, Jesus could not belong to more than one race; he could not live everywhere. He came, however, to enable all the human race to know themselves as part of the family of God. He came as a Jew, and to begin with his ministry was to the lost sheep of the house of Israel; but he came also to break down the wall of partition between Jew and Gentile. 'There is neither Jew nor Greek, there is neither bond nor free, there is neither male nor female; for ye are all one in Christ Jesus' (Gal. 3.28). Remarks like that must have sounded devastating to the Jews in those days. As the first Adam was the father of all men according to the flesh, so the second Adam would reunite all mankind. The vision of the heavenly city in the Book of Revelation shows a similar thought; in it 'a great multitude of all nations and kindred and peoples and tongues stood before the throne and before the Lamb' (Rev. 7.9).

3 Come and see

Unfortunately this attitude, expressed by Nathanael is easier to describe (and even to recognize in ourselves) than to cure. All too easily we prejudge an individual because he belongs to a certain grouping, or, the other way round, we are prejudiced against a whole group because of one of its members. Again and again in the Gospels we are warned not to prejudge but to look more deeply. Again and again (not just in the Gospels) we are reminded that God looks not at the outward appearance but at the heart. The reply to Nathanael's outburst of scorn remains the only answer, 'Come and see.' If we want better relations with, say, a Christian denomination from which we are separated, the answer applies, 'Come and see.' In towns where there are many racial and religious groups, there is only one right way forward. Unless their neighbours come and see, to get to know and understand them better, divided communities will continue. Equally if we believe we have a faith which is true, and a fellowship which is loyal to its Lord, we must be ready to invite others to 'Come and see.'

EPIPHANY 3

Obedience

John 2.5 (AV) *'Whatsoever he saith unto you, do it.'*

The story of the turning of the water into wine at the wedding at Cana in Galilee is very familiar. It is the first of such signs recorded in the fourth Gospel. The effect on the steward of the feast is described, 'You have kept the best wine until now.' The effect on the disciples is described; they believed on him. But let us try to see it through the eyes of the servants who for some reason had evidently brought the problem to Mary. After a cryptic few words with Jesus, Mary turns to the servants and tells them to do whatever Jesus says. So they go to him for instructions. The first of the two instructions must have seemed very odd, to say the least. By all means fill the water-pots with water, but what on earth has that got to do with the immediate problem which was a shortage of wine, not water? Still, they do it and come back for further orders. 'Now draw and take to the steward of the feast.' The stewards must have been staggered. They knew it was water they had drawn, and what would happen to them if they now took water to the steward? Instant dismissal?

1 Obedience follows trust

Let us put ourselves in the position of those servants. Quite honestly, would you have done it? Even if they could pass the blame, either on to Mary or Jesus, half the miracle is that they did what they were asked. There must have been something about Jesus which so affected them that they were prepared to carry out such an order. But they did what they were asked, and the divine power was revealed. We have no reason to think that this was anything other than their first meeting with Jesus. Their trust in him which led them to obey is amazing. Is our trust in him even remotely comparable?

2 When obedience challenges

This is far from the only example of a situation where Jesus asks someone to do something beyond their sense of earthly reason or possibility. 'Launch out into the deep and let down your nets for a draught,' and we know what the experienced fisherman answered – with the half-believing addition 'nevertheless at thy word I will let down the net'. Again, to the centurion who had travelled a long way to fetch Jesus to heal his son, who was desperately ill, Jesus says, 'Go thy way; thy son liveth;' and the man believed the word that Jesus had spoken to him, and he went his way. That must have taken some doing. The man at the Pool of Bethesda was told to get up and walk; he must have thought it impossible, but he did it. This can happen to us. A situation arises and there seems to be no reasonable or possible way out. What we are told by others, or have some inner conviction to think is the right thing to do, may seem useless or impossible. But there is only one answer for the Christian: 'whatsoever he saith unto you, do it'. The prayer by Bishop Westcott is relevant: 'When we have done what thou hast given us to do, help us, O God our Saviour, to leave the issue to thy wisdom.'

The issue at Cana in Galilee was that the power of God was revealed; the same applied at the lakeside, at the pool of Bethesda, and to the centurion's son at Capernaum. This is so often the way of God. The channel of his power is often the obedience of man. It is not so much that God cannot work without our obedience, but that we are privileged to be his fellow workers. We may have all the sympathy in the world for the plague-stricken people in some remote country, but if man does nothing they will continue sick and hungry. If this is true, then a special place in our prayers must be given so that we may know his will. 'Today if ye will hear his voice, harden not your hearts.' Perhaps if we knew that some dramatic demonstration of God's power would result from our obedience, we might be more ready both to listen and obey. (Compare Naaman: 2 Kings 5.13). Often God's demand on us in quite small and homely. But the message of Cana still holds good, 'Whatsoever he saith unto you, do it.'

EPIPHANY 4

Conversion of St Paul

Philippians 3.14 '*I press toward the mark of the prize of our high calling in Christ.*'

It is quite remarkable how many records there are in the New Testament of men and women who met Jesus once, but of whom we do not hear again. Quite apart from the various people whom he healed, the woman taken in adultery whose life was spared when Jesus said, 'Let him that is without sin cast the first stone,' or the woman at the well, there were others who could never forget the day when they came face to face with Jesus. Caiaphas, Pontius Pilate and others at the time of the trial and crucifixion are only known because of one day in their lives. In a sense this is to be expected. As Christians, we would say that the most important day in anyone's life is the day they came face to face with Christ. With St Paul, the situation is quite different; we know a certain amount about him before his conversion and a great deal more about what he did afterwards.

1 The road from Damascus

Many of the people of whom we read in the Gospels were anxious to meet Jesus; the centurion from Capernaum, the blind beggars and men like Zacchaeus, positively sought him out. Saul of Tarsus wished to have nothing to do with him, but rather to persecute any of his followers. It was the risen, living Christ, who sought him out, and that meeting on the road to Damascus was the turning-point, the conversion, of his life. In some ways it looks like an example of sudden conversion but the effects even of such a sudden experience take a long time to work themselves out. The period between a D-Day, a day of decision, and a V-Day, a day of victory, may be a long one. Here in his letter to the Christians in Philippi, St Paul is describing the process of growth in the likeness of Christ. Just as once he had sought out and pursued the Jews who believed in Jesus, so now he seeks out and pursues the 'prize of our high calling in Christ'. There was a long road ahead for Paul from Damascus. Instead of his persecution of the Christian Jews, he was attacked by the non-Christian Jews; he lists some of the hardships, beatings, imprisonment and shipwrecks he suffered. Nor was the struggle only outward. 'The good that I would, I do not; but the evil that I would not, that I do.'

2 A life-time struggle

In much the same way, the path ahead was only made clear in short stages. At his conversion the Lord said to him, 'Go into the city and you will be told what you have to do;' not till three days after he got there were his eyes opened. His path then was not easy for there was opposition both from Jews and Christians. Should he go back home, to Tarsus? Later came the call to Antioch, with Barnabas. At each stage, all the way to his final destination in Rome, there had to be a constant readiness to change course. Sudden conversion? Yes, but followed by a lifetime of new decisions, and a lifetime of inward struggle between the old self and the new man in Christ.

3 Build-up and follow-up

All this, in different circumstances, is true for us today. Conversion is not complete on the first day, but needs to be renewed all through life. In *The Pilgrim's Progress*, at the end of his journey Christian is warned that there is a path to hell just before the final gate to heaven. Conversion may be the start of our sanctification, that slow transformation of ourselves into the likeness of Christ. At no point can we say that we 'have attained'. So also with our sense of vocation, there must indeed be an initial decision to follow the leading of Christ, to go through life with him as our guide, and also our strength. But every occasion of major decision – our Confirmation day, our wedding day and, for the clergy, the day of Ordination – has a long build-up and a long follow-up. None of this takes away from the importance of the decision on the day itself. Perhaps then the conversion of St Paul is not so different from our experience as it might seem at first sight.

Seeking a sign

> Matthew 12.38 (NEB) '*Some of the doctors of the law and the Pharisees said, 'Master, we should like you to show us a sign.'*

The sign that was asked for was more than some strange act of healing; they wanted proof that Jesus was genuine, and not in league with the powers of evil. When he had been accused of casting out devils by Beelzebub, the prince of devils, he had reminded them that exorcism was practised among themselves. 'By whom do your sons cast them out?' They were looking for a sign of a higher order. A prophecy of a strange happening in the future which could be verified would do. Was not this the test of a true prophet? Elijah and the three-year drought, and the prophecies of Jeremiah, might well have come to mind.

1 Jesus would not tempt God

The temptation to show a convincing sign must have come often to Jesus. The temptation by the devil in the wilderness was to do something which would convince everybody (including himself?) that he was the Son of God; casting himself down from the pinnacle of the temple would suffice. Such a sign might have made people take notice; on the other hand, they would be likely to remember the sign and forget the teaching. Herod had hoped to see some miracle done, and was disappointed. But the temptation must have come most strongly at the crucifixion, 'If you are the Son of God, come down from the cross and we will believe.' But we believe because he stayed up. On the other hand the resurrection of Jesus has been for many the assurance which has established their faith.

2 Jesus would not be tempted by men

With all the miracles that Jesus did perform, it might seem that his refusal to give a sign when asked by the Pharisees is rather confusing, if not inconsistent. But all the miracles came from the initiative of Jesus himself, to relieve hunger or sickness or sorrow. The demand for a sign was to tempt God, to put God to the test. The sinfulness of this is that it is an attempt to reverse the roles of God and man. When you put anybody or anything to the test, you are master and they are servant; you are examiner and not pupil. God is creator, man is created; God is master and lord, man is servant. It is God who is law-giver; man is called to obedience. Jesus, we believe, was both human and divine. Because he was human, he would not tempt God, asserting his divinity and putting God to the test; because he was divine, he would not submit to being put to the test himself. Here indeed we touch on one of the deepest mysteries of the faith. As St Paul puts it (Phil. 2.6) Jesus did not treat his equality with God as something to be grasped.

3 Signs following

Yet we all like, or would like, some assurance that our faith is well-founded. On some occasion, perhaps, our prayers have been 'wonderfully answered'; we did not pray in order to put God to the test but because we were very concerned about something. The answer to our prayers strengthened the weak faith with which we prayed; some faith had to be there for the prayer to be genuine. More often, however, we recognize the signs after the event rather than at the time. Moments of revelation may come, but for most people are rare; they are certainly not given as something to be made public, things about which to boast (2 Cor. 12.1–10). We all read about, and may have encountered, examples of remarkable healing taking place through the laying on of hands with prayer. The danger of the person exercising it becoming a 'cult-figure' is always present; equally great is the dangerous temptation to others without faith to look for a miracle. We must never despair, if we have faith; we must never presume, as though the power belonged not to God but to his human agents. If at any time some assurance has been given us, let us thank God; but always we need to remember that we are called to walk by faith and not by sight.

EPIPHANY 6

Images of God

> Isaiah 40.18 (AV) *'To whom then will ye liken God? Or what likeness will ye compare unto him?'*

1 Images for worship banned

The second of the Commandments is quite plain. We are to worship God himself and not any image or assumed likeness of God. The Old Testament is full of reminders that idols are powerless. 'They have mouths and speak not; eyes have they and see not . . .' (Ps. 115.4–8). The true God, the God who made heaven and earth and all living creatures, is too great to be represented by a model. Many of the words we use to address God express the difference between him and anything earthly.

> Immortal, invisible, God only wise,
> In light inaccessible hid from our eyes.

Isaiah has the same thought 'As the heavens are higher than the earth, so are my ways higher than your ways, and my thoughts than your thoughts' (Isa. 55.9). All this is clearly very true, but are we not in danger of being so vague both in our thinking and language that we really do not know what we are doing when we worship or say our prayers. In fact, of course, the Old

Testament (let alone the New) is full of imagery to help to give a picture of God. He is ruler and king and, as he is all-seeing and all-knowing, is able to judge fairly and justly. From time to time, the mercy of God is described and, indeed, his actions can be compared with those of a father (e.g. Ps. 103). What God is like can only be inferred from what he does.

2 Pointers are helpful

In the teaching of Jesus we have many parables which are used to point to the ways of God. That is just what they do. They are pointers, not detailed descriptions. They are stories complete in themselves which help us to see truths of a higher order. The meaning of the parables was by no means obvious to all his hearers at the time. Indeed, we read in several places that after Jesus had taught the people publicly, he then explained the parables to the disciples privately. There is also a sense in which all the parables have to be taken together; they are pointers to the ways of God from many different directions. What we have to be careful not to do is to treat the parables as though they were images or pictures of God, and to press all the details.

But, if it is wrong, that is to say breaking the second Commandment, to make an image of God, is all religious art to be condemned? Is all imagery from illustrations in children's books to the masterpieces of Raphael or Leonardo da Vinci wicked? Perhaps, on the other hand, religious art gives us some help in understanding the parables. None of the artists or sculptors had seen Jesus, indeed nowhere are we given any hint as to his appearance. All they can do is to use their imagination and then express their thoughts. They are not saying, 'this is how you have to picture Jesus,' but rather, 'this picture helps me to think of Jesus'. I have to admit that some stained glass windows of the resurrection and the ascension do not help me at all; but maybe they help others. In much the same way, the picture-language in the Book of the Revelation of St John is not meant to be a detailed description of heaven, but pointers to

37

the truths of judgement, and of the sovereignty of Christ. There is a story told of a missionary in Africa, to whom the Africans paid no attention; when he pressed them to discover the reason they told him that his description of God was all wrong. 'In the first place, she's black.'

3 Reminder of God's presence

Religious art, the parables and even the sacraments themselves are earthly things which turn our hearts and minds to God. Whether it is a cross on the altar or a sanctuary light or a stained glass window, when you go into a church you are reminded of the presence of God. His presence is everywhere though it may be focused and therefore more easily realized in certain ways and certain places. The sacrament of Holy Communion is a particular instance, but it is good to recall the words of Bishop Westcott that 'whenever things temporal reach out into the eternal and carry us with them to God, there is a sacrament'. All these things point us to God, but God himself is beyond all description; and worship must be offered only to God, and never to the earthly things—even though they point to him.

NINTH SUNDAY BEFORE EASTER
(SEPTUAGESIMA)

Teaching with authority

Matthew 7.28–29 (Post-Communion sentence (ASB))
'*The people were astounded at the teaching of Jesus; for he taught them with authority.*'

1 Christ's authority

Jesus had no official standing, like the Scribes or Pharisees, to lend weight to his teaching. It was only natural that every now and then his teaching would clash with that of the authorities. A free-lance Evangelist today may find quite a few hearers, but is likely to be regarded as an outsider by the Church authorities. Indeed the Churches have spent a great deal of time and thought recently (ARCIC Reports, etc) trying to understand and define the basis of authority; scripture, tradition and reason all have their place. All these are intertwined. The scriptures arose out of a living Church; in their turn they determine its life. But the authority of Jesus was both recognized and challenged. At the cleansing of the Temple (Matt. 21.23–27) the chief priests and elders directly asked, 'By what authority doest thou these things? and who gave thee this authority?'

The weeks which led up to the trial and crucifixion are dominated by this question. 'Who is this?' asked the crowd as Jesus entered Jerusalem, triumphantly yet humbly, on Palm Sunday. 'Where do you come from?' and again, 'Are you the King of the Jews?' asked Pilate. 'Art thou the Christ, the Son of the Blessed?' asked the High Priest. It was not just because of the works of healing that people wanted to know the source of his power; though his curing of the blind and of lepers went beyond the range of 'faith-healing'. It was his teaching which stood out in contrast with that of the Scribes and Pharisees. He

39

even went beyond the words of scripture; 'Ye have heard that it hath been said . . . but I say unto you.' Think of this in modern terms. An unordained preacher stands up and says, 'You know that in the Bible it is written . . . but I say to you. . . .' Even in our divided Church, he would not get very far; we might let him go on, so long as he confined himself to the passers-by in Hyde Park, otherwise we would ignore him.

2 Christ's hidden authority

Jesus could not be ignored. That lies behind the theme of Lent, Good Friday and Easter. It should be the burden of the message of the whole Church to the whole world, not least to the vast majority in our country who call themselves Christians but ignore the Christ whose name they bear. There was something in the teaching of Jesus which demanded attention. Some of it must have sounded outrageous, 'Love your enemies,' for example. The Christ of the Sermon on the Mount is scarcely 'Gentle Jesus, meek and mild' of the children's hymn. Yet for all the apparent extremes in his teaching, and the seemingly impossible ideals he set out, there was an authority about him which everybody recognized, a sincerity and a ring of truth which no one could gainsay – we know nothing about his appearance or his tone of voice, but what was it that made the disciples forsake all and follow him after such brief contact and limited understanding? Throughout the Gospel record it is clear that there was something about Jesus which commanded attention and demanded response.

3 The Christian's hidden authority

In a similar, though greatly reduced, way the same is true of many Christian people down the ages and today. They believe in Christ, they proclaim him to others and something about them makes their words ring true. There is an integrity and a depth which others note; there is a reflection in their own lives of the Christ whom they serve and proclaim. They are not only Christian but Christlike. If the Christian faith produces people like that, there must be something in it. Holiness, which is Christlikeness, carries its own authority; confronted with it, people are impelled to take notice. The God of whom Jesus spoke was no distant or strange power; he was the Father, always near at hand, in whose love he lived and moved and had his being. Jesus did not have to pass any examination in biblical knowledge; he knew the God he talked about. And the people were astounded at his teaching; for he taught them with authority.

EIGHTH SUNDAY BEFORE EASTER

Faithfulness in little things

> 2 Kings 5.13 (NEB) '*If the prophet had bidden you do something difficult, would you not do it?*'
> Luke 16.10 (AV) '*He that is faithful in that which is least is faithful also in much.*'

1 Public recognition

Naaman was an important man. His successes as Commander-in-Chief were widely acclaimed. All ranks would be expected to salute him. But Elisha did not even come out of the house to greet him, even though he had arrived with a great procession of chariots and horses. To do what Elisha's messenger said was beneath his dignity; fortunately for him, he was persuaded otherwise.

Nowadays with all the facilities available to press and television, it is possible for the smallest action of the greatest person to be universally known. The Pope picks up a baby and gives it a kiss, and the whole world sees it. At the other end of the scale, it is a matter of understandable pride if an otherwise undistinguished person gets his name in the news for doing something out of the ordinary (and good, of course).

2 Habitual actions

Most of us, however, are very ordinary people and most of the things we do are very ordinary things, often repeated daily. The average housewife does the washing up rather more than a thousand times a year. In our religious life, much the same applies; we are equally creatures of habit in matters of our faith as in other things. Yet in many ways that which is not seen by the world, our daily time of private prayer for example, may be a far greater factor in our lives than the visible practice of our faith on Sundays. Even the latter can become an unexciting matter of habit, however good the habit. I recall a Presbyterian minister, many years ago, saying, 'You Anglicans value the Holy Communion so much, you seem to have it on every possible occasion; we value it so much, we only have it four times a year.' Habits may change, but there is no ideal half-way house.

Charles Wesley expresses this truth in the last verse of one of his hymns. 'Ready for all thy perfect will, my acts of faith and love repeat.' The oft-repeated trivial expressions of love help to keep a marriage alive, and similar things between parents and children contribute to family solidarity. Home would not be the same if we changed our habits even every year. Charles Wesley is right, there is a lot of repetition in the Christian life; but the acts which we repeat again and again make us what we are. If we gave them up, thinking they have become mere formalities, we should become different people. We may, for example, be in the habit of saying grace before meals; even if we are not consciously thinking about our dependence on God each time, the habit is a reminder that we ought to be grateful to him.

In ten days' time we shall be in the season of Lent, a traditional time for checking up on our religious practice and either 'giving something up' or perhaps doing something extra. Don't make it so drastic that you cannot wait for Easter in order to get back to normal; you will only be disheartened if you fail, or painfully proud of yourself if you succeed. The more invisible the habit is to the world at large the better it will be. What has happened to those people for whom you once prayed, but now are never mentioned, God-children, former colleagues, school friends and former neighbours? Make a list of forty of them, and pray for a different one each day during Lent. Or maybe once a week, we might do an untraceable act of kindness – a small gift at a sick man's house when nobody is looking, or even an anonymous donation to some good cause. God perceives what the world cannot see, he knows the secret thoughts of our hearts and can use small and apparently insignificant things as the means of our health and spiritual growth. He that is faithful in that which is least, is faithful also in much.

SEVENTH SUNDAY BEFORE EASTER

Mercy and truth

> Psalm 85.10 (AV) *'Mercy and truth are met together; righteousness and peace have kissed each other.'*

1 Apparent opposites

The prerogative of mercy, in our English legal system, belongs to the Crown and is exercised by the Home Secretary; in the days of the death penalty, it was a very heavy responsibility. Justice says, 'You must suffer this'; mercy says 'but I will let you off'. Seen in this light, justice and mercy appear to be opposites. The woman who had been taken in the act of adultery provided the Pharisees with an excellent example by which to put Jesus to the test. It might sound attractive for him to talk about mercy, but here was a blatant case of sin; the law of Moses was clear, she should be stoned. Did Jesus put himself above the law? The reply of Jesus was a reminder to them that no one is without sin, and an assurance to the woman that no one is beyond God's mercy.

2 The God of natural law

Justice, law, righteousness and truth are marks of a whole area of thinking and behaviour. They are characteristics of God. They are evidence and signs of reliability and are praised as such throughout the Bible. God is the source of all law and order; he does not change; he has made the round world so fast that it cannot be moved. Without putting it in that sort of language, the reliability of God is the basis of all natural science; because things have behaved in a certain way in the past, we rely on their future behaviour being the same. It would be a hopeless world to live in if this were not so. 'While the earth remaineth, seed-time and harvest, and cold and heat, and summer and winter, and day and night shall not cease' (Gen. 8.22).

3 The God of moral law

In addition to being the source of all natural law, God is the source of all moral law. In this also we believe he does not change. If murder or theft or covetousness were declared to be wrong once, they are still wrong. Obviously we have to use some common sense to distinguish between laws in the Old Testament relating to local conditions at a certain time, and

those which are of general application. Clearly also much of the
message of the prophets relates to the application of a general
moral law to a particular set of circumstances. The basis of the
moral law in the Old Testament is not a division of actions and
attitudes into good and bad, or right and wrong, but into those
which please or offend the living God. The living God does not
change; his power and his will are the same throughout all ages.

4 The God of mercy

But in addition to being the source of all law, God is a God of
mercy. 'To the Lord our God belong mercies and forgivenesses,
though we have rebelled against him' (Dan. 9.9). That which is
declared and described in the Old Testament of the kindness
and mercy of God is revealed in the New Testament in the
person of Christ. He came to reveal that God loves us in spite of
our sins, and to take upon himself the consequence of our sin. It
is a commonplace to say that God hates sin but loves the sinner,
but it is a pointer to an important truth. The moral law is the
personal will of an unchanging God. Sin is not so much a failure
to maintain a certain standard, but an offence against the person
of God. To put it rather crudely, we shall not arrive in heaven
because we have attained a certain pass mark in moral
behaviour, but because God wants us to be with him for ever.

5 The opposites reconciled

St Paul describes at some length this tension between law and
grace, between righteousness, truth, law and order on the one
hand and mercy, kindness, peace and love on the other hand. If
grace and forgiveness are so wonderful, 'shall we continue in sin
that grace may abound?' (Rom. 6.1). Obviously not. But the
reasoning is clear; 'to whom ye yield yourselves servants to
obey, his servants ye are whom ye obey' (Rom. 6.16). Morality
is a matter of personal relationship, it springs from our love of a

personal God. Looked at impersonally, forgiveness would seem to be condoning sin; if we can be sure of forgiveness at the end, why bother to keep the law? Seen personally, sin is doing and being what God, who loves us, does not want us to do and to be. But God still loves in spite of what we have done and have become as a result. In him mercy and truth, love and unchanging will, are met together. There is no changing of his will; there is no limit to his mercy.

LENT 1

Lost sheep

Isaiah 53.6 (AV) *'All we like sheep have gone astray.'*

Conductors of Handel's Messiah differ in their way of interpreting this chorus. I recall one conductor telling us not to sound too cheerful about it, for it is a serious matter. At a recent performance, when the chorus was sung rather fast and very cheerfully, I mentioned this to the conductor afterwards. 'But that is the point, as I see it. The sheep were enjoying themselves; it was the shepherd who was worried,' he replied.

1 *Three kinds of loss*

The three great parables in St Luke's Gospel, chapter 15, tell of three kinds of loss. The sheep wandered off, probably enjoying itself at first; it was not naughty, for it didn't know better. Maybe it felt lost later and bleated accordingly. The anxious shepherd looked for it and found it. The coin was lost, and knew nothing about it; the owner, who may not have been careful enough, was anxious and had to do all the looking. A coin cannot bleat like a sheep to tell you where it is. The prodigal son was lost through his own deliberate fault. He knew what he was doing, thoroughly enjoyed himself at first, had his fill and then found his life empty. He had a good home and a good father, and valued neither. It was hunger which first prompted him to come back; penitence came later. (Compare the confession in the ASB 'We have sinned ... through negligence, through weakness, through our own deliberate fault.'). All three were lost, but equally all three lost something themselves. The sheep lost the security of the flock, the coin lost its usefulness and purchasing power, the son lost the intimacy and active membership of his home.

2 Lost to the Church

There are plenty of sheep, coins and sons lost to the Church today. Where are all those who have been confirmed in the last ten years? Some have just wandered off; the grass in the next field looked greener, and the fence was broken. The other ninety-nine sheep did not notice that one was missing. Perhaps the distraction was a boyfriend or girlfriend who belonged to no church; or a gang with quite other interests. After all 'Can you not be just as good a Christian without going to church?' But the flock is incomplete, and often has not noticed the absence of the lost sheep. But the shepherd is worried.

Or again, like the coin, some are lost not through their own fault. Not everyone has as good a home or Christian background as we may have had. Or is it that we have not made the fellowship of the church attractive enough? Perhaps the fault lies with their parents, or with ourselves.

There are, of course, some lost sons who have knowingly and deliberately left the Christian family. However anxious or concerned we may be, they will make their own decision as to whether and when to return. Perhaps they think the door will be shut if they do. If they have physically wandered off, how are they to know? Perhaps the Mothers' Union 'Message Home' scheme could be matched in other fields.

These sheep, coins and sons (and daughters!) are lost and have themselves lost something; but so have we. The flock is incomplete; the ability to get things done is weakened; the family circle is broken. Have we noticed their absence, and are we as worried as the shepherd? His anxiety is unlimited, shown by his willingness to die for us; the good shepherd lays down his life for the sheep. The Son of Man is come to seek and to save that which was lost. He has already done all that needs to be done for the saving, but he looks to us to share in the task of seeking.

LENT 2

No half-way house

> Matthew 12.30: Luke 11.23 (AV) *'He who is not with me is against me: and he that gathereth not with me, scattereth.'*

It would seem that Jesus deliberately tried to make people come to a decision about him. Unlike some (? most) of us, he was not content to live a quiet and peaceful life, avoiding all extremes and being obviously in love and charity with his neighbours. He revealed his power and authority; in his teaching he claimed an authority even greater than scripture. He would not compromise, and eventually the Jewish authorities had to decide whether to accept his claims or else to silence him. The one thing they could not do was to ignore him.

1 Spectators

If Jesus came again today, would things be very different? Would we be shocked if our rather lovely prayers, 'Be present at our table, Lord', or even 'Come to my heart, Lord Jesus, there is room in my heart for thee', were to be answered? Perhaps we like to skip over verses like 'I am not come to bring peace but a sword', and move quickly to the next chapter. All of which reveals the very obvious fact that we are a generation of spectators; events as diverse as a royal wedding, or a World Cup Final are watched by hundreds of millions all over the world. Most of us probably watched and enjoyed both. This is not in any way to scorn the media or to blame them for making us into spectators; we were spectators already and the media enables us to see more of the game. Indeed, with world-wide coverage, they bring to our immediate notice events and issues otherwise beyond our knowledge. In a way never possible before, we can rejoice with those that do rejoice and weep with them that weep.

2 Non-involvement

But the problem goes much deeper. Most of us like being spectators and (quite rightly) would rather have a sporting fixture than a fighting fixture with another country. This applies also to our outward religious activity. Quite apart from the majority of English Christians who have goodwill but no active involvement in church life, those of us who are church-goers are just that – churchgoers. We may, of course, become active church members and some churches multiply activities from choirs to youth clubs to help their members get involved. I wonder what the equivalent was in the early Church, or among the Jews at the time of our Lord. Dorcas was undoubtedly chairperson of the local needlework guild. But are not most of us glad that we do not live in the trouble spots of which we read? We would rather have race relations between 'them and them' than between 'him and me.' The criminal world, the violent world, the world of excess, greed and hatred, we want to avoid. Fortunately most of us are able to avoid it, and keep ourselves fully occupied 'supporting' the church.

The season of Lent, leading up to Good Friday and Easter, is a reminder that this is not the way of God. The world of sin was the very world into which Christ came. In his teaching, he made it clear that he had come to call sinners to repentance. His coming was the measure of his love. In the old film *The Green Pastures*, the angel Gabriel is depicted as trying to dissuade the Son of God from visiting the earth because all humankind was evil, they would be better destroyed. The reply, 'But I love them, I must go', faithfully reflects the mind of Christ. God is not a distant passive spectator, but an active helper and redeemer. In all our affliction, he is afflicted. Love spells involvement. The one thing the priest and the Levite on the road from Jerusalem to Jericho did not want was to get involved. We often feel the same; 'I'm glad I'm not mixed up with that lot.' But Jesus deliberately came, to show us the pain that our sinfulness causes to God.

The teaching of Jesus is quite clear, love means involvement. 'He that is not with me is against me.' With Christ there cannot be disinterested spectators; we are either for him or against him.

LENT 3

The Annunciation

Luke 1.48 (AV) *Behold, from henceforth all generations shall call me blessed.*

1 A happy mother

How rich and full of meaning is that word, 'blessed'! It includes, among other things, the sense of happiness; it includes ·

also the sense of having been given something, rather than having earned it. Both these senses would have applied to Mary. However great the responsibility, she must have been supremely happy and gone round with an expectant mother's smile. The very human story of her visit to Elizabeth certainly suggests this.

2 A pained mother

Of course, there are two sides to everything and Mary was warned that she would have sad and heavy times as well. 'A sword shall pierce through thine own heart also.' It is too easy for us to think of Mary in terms of Lady Day and Christmas, and to forget all that must have happened after. There was all the caring for the infant, bringing up the boy through teenage, the anxieties during his ministry leading up to her sad watch by the Cross – loving, but unable to help. The pain of that moment would have been in proportion to her love, and how much she must have loved her son.

3 A real mother

Yet, however much we may exalt the Blessed Virgin Mary and call her 'Mother of God' as an assurance that her son was indeed God incarnate, we do well to remember that her motherhood was very real and earthly. She was not just a human tool or instrument used by God to enable the Incarnation to take place. Her task as mother went on and on. Indeed, the reality of her motherhood is part of our assurance of the reality of the manhood of Jesus. 'He was little, weak and helpless; tears and smiles like us he knew', and she had to attend to him. The exaltation of Mary is reflected in many works of art, both paintings and statuary. It is hard to envisage the Madonna of medieval art getting down to the weekly (or daily) washing consequent on the birth of a child. Nor does one always see that happiness breaking through, which the Magnificat implies. Yet she was mother, not just nurse. The child Jesus was her child. God chose her and trusted her.

4 A trusted mother

'Trust;' what a wealth of meaning there is in that word also. Every child is created to be a child of God, and every parent is God's trustee for one of his children. This thought lifts parenthood as a vocation to a very high level. Responsibility and dignity, happiness and holiness go hand in hand.

An appeal

How sad it is that the varying degrees of honour accorded to the Blessed Virgin Mary should have been the cause of division among Christians. What is important is that we should thank God that he chose her for such a responsible role; that we should rejoice with those that do rejoice, and so catch even something of her joy when we sing the Magnificat. Remembrance of her can perhaps prompt us to pray for all mothers today, on whom rests so much responsibility for the spirit of the world tomorrow.

LENT 4

Seeing and perceiving

> Matthew 17.5 (Post Communion sentence (ASB)
> '*This is my Son, my Beloved in whom is all my delight;
> listen to him.*'

The Transfiguration of Jesus

It may seem strange, at first sight, to have the transfiguration as the theme of a Sunday in the middle of Lent. In one sense, however, this should have prepared the three disciples, Peter, James and John, for the events of the crucifixion and resurrection about which Jesus spoke to them afterwards. The transfiguration is described as occurring after Jesus had asked the disciples who they, and others, thought he was; in other words, after the confession of Peter, 'Thou art the Christ.' The resurrection occurred when the disciples were sad and the meaning had gone out of life; even when it came to the last appearance (Matt. 28.17) 'some doubted'. We shall never know 'exactly what happened' at either event, but it is clear that on this occasion the three chosen disciples saw how much greater than Moses or one of the prophets Jesus really was.

2 The transfiguration of the disciples' view

At the resurrection appearances, the disciples had to ask themselves, 'Is this really Jesus?'; that question did not arise now. What they saw was Jesus all right, but they were able to see or perceive more. This Jesus, with whom they had been walking and talking for so long, was more than just another man. What they saw was the same, yet different; a fellow man of the earth, yet filled with a glory 'out of this world'.

There is indeed all the difference in the world between seeing

53

and perceiving. What a bridegroom sees in his bride—the embodiment of love – is so much more than what the world sees. What a young couple see in their first-born babe is a lot more than seven pounds of pink flesh; there is the fruit of their love, a trust more precious than words can express, with a life of its own yet more 'theirs' than any jointly-owned possession. In some such way, the experience of the transfiguration enabled Peter, James and John to see in Jesus so much more than met the eye.

3 Other transfigurations

(a) Suffering

The particular event described in the Gospels happened once only, and in only one place. But God can and does transfigure many of the events in our lives. Sickness and suffering, with many earthly accompaniments which we try to hide from the eyes (and noses) of the casual visitor, can be transfigured by God. The sick person can see his disability as the occasion of so much kindness on the part of others. During his sickness he discovers, sometimes to his surprise, who his friends really are. This can work in reverse. There are some sick and handicapped people whose courage and cheerfulness restore our own faith in human nature when we ourselves are feeling depressed.

(b) Homes

Then again the presence of Christ can transfigure a home. It cannot easily be described, but you can feel the difference. Outwardly the ingredients are the same as any other house, but the harmony is different, even if the outsider cannot tell what (who?) is the cause of the difference.

(c) Death

Above all, the presence of Christ can and does transfigure death, both for the dying person and for his friends. All the physical accompaniments of death point to it as the end of a life – marriage, parenthood, work, friendships are coming to an end. Instinctively, we look back rather than forward. But the assurance of the presence of Christ transforms this. It is not that the dying person is leaving us to be with Christ; he is with Christ already, and so are we. The limitations of space and time, imposed by an earthly body, are done away. Death is indeed an open gate and not a closed door.

Conclusion

Seen in this light, the transfiguration is not just a remarkable incident in the past, but an assurance that when Christ is present life is transformed.

PASSION SUNDAY—LENT 5

If it be possible

> Matthew 26.39 (AV) '*O my Father, if it be possible, let this cup pass from me; nevertheless, not as I will, but as thou wilt.*'

1 Jesus' experience of tension

There is a real sense in which half the passion of our Lord was enacted in the Garden of Gethsemane. Jesus could see what lay ahead, and he would not have been human if he had not shrunk from it. Few incidents in the record of our Lord's life reveal more clearly both the tension of the human and the divine, and the unity of them in Jesus. The tension had been growing ever since he had set his face to go up to Jerusalem, knowing full well that this would mean his death. There was no turning back, if his task of revealing the divine love and will was to be complete. Equally the tension was not over, once the decision was made; it grew until the final cry of desolation on the cross. This scene in Gethsemane reveals what must have been going on for some time.

2 Jesus wills to do God's will

The wording of the prayer of Jesus is worth noting. He calls on God as Father; the cry of desolation on the cross (quotation or no quotation) is the only occasion when Jesus addresses God other than as Father. The record in St Mark and St Matthew reads 'if it be possible'; St Luke is typically more gentle 'if thou be willing'. The human terror is clearer in Mark and Matthew, 'Is it not possible to reveal the Father's love without going through this?', coupled with a readiness to do the will of the Father. It is so easy for us to recite the Lord's prayer, 'Thy will be done,' without realizing the depth of meaning it can have. On the other hand there is not the first suggestion of any sense of resignation, or conflict of will between his own and that of the Father. On the contrary, though the horror remained, there is a victorious determination from this point; St Luke puts it that in the garden an angel appeared to him to strengthen him.

3 Our shallow appreciation of God's will

It is easy to look on this incident as an example of unanswered prayer, that is to say of a prayer to which the answer was 'No.' Often we wish for something to happen and pray for it to happen, but it does not. If we have little faith, we say that our prayer was not answered; if we have a little more faith, we adjust ourselves to the conclusion that the answer was 'No', and that God knows best what is good for us and for the world. Too often the phrase, 'Thy will be done', is added not exactly as a let-out, but as an act of resignation because of our ignorance of God's will. Sometimes, it should be added, our requests are not granted because of the evil actions of others. In times of war and conflict, very many prayers are not answered in the way they were made because the sin of man made the requests impossible. But it would be almost blasphemy to put 'Thy will be done' on the tombstones of the victims of road accidents, political oppression or murder.

4 Jesus' acceptance of God's will

The prayer in the Garden of Gethsemane takes us into an area of mystery. Was the crucifixion the will of God? Is God like that, willing the cruel murder of the innocent? If so, is he the kind of God to whom we would want to address our prayers? If Jesus were not himself divine, if he were an 'other' person created by God to fulfil this role, there would be only one possible answer. But if, as we believe, Jesus was God made man we can see deeper into the mystery. The will of man is to avoid suffering if possible; the will of God is to accept the suffering caused by the sinful will of man. It is this tension, human and divine, that we see in Gethsemane going on in the heart of Jesus who was both human and divine. It was not the crucifixion, but the acceptance of it, that was the will of God. It is in that acceptance that there is seen the victory of the cross, the victory of divine love unbroken by the concentrated sin of man. That victory is foreshadowed in this prayer, revealed on Calvary and sealed by the resurrection.

Ye are the temple of God

1 Corinthians 3.16 (AV) *'Know ye not that ye are the temple of God, and that the Spirit of God dwelleth in you?*

1 A disturbing historical event

The entry of Jesus into Jerusalem on Palm Sunday brought to a head both the popular support and acclaim, and also the official opposition of the Jewish authorities. It also revealed the weakness of the former and the strength of the latter. The same crowd that cheered 'Hosanna to the Son of David' on the Sunday, were responding to the prompting of the chief priests and others (e.g. Matt. 27.20) four days later and shouting, 'Let him be crucified.' The popular acclaim might have prodded the authorities into action, had it been necessary; the actions of Jesus in the temple did it for them. Evidently the chief priests had little difficulty in harnessing the support of the weak-willed crowd. The power of propaganda was evidently not very different in those days from what it is now. Jesus was not an official or authorized Rabbi or elder. If the establishment was to continue in peace, the actions of Jesus in the temple could not be tolerated. Jesus was not content, as it were, to sit down and enjoy the cheering of the crowd; it was he who threw the challenge to the authorities, at the cost of his life.

2 A disturbing up-dating of that event

Is it possible to up-date this event and bring it into the present? We do it at Christmas, for example, in the hymn 'O little town of Bethlehem.' The last verse reads:

O holy child of Bethlehem
Descend to us, we pray;
Cast out our sin, and enter in:
Be born in us today.

That sounds lovely at Christmas, but what would be the equivalent for Palm Sunday? If it were known in advance, the souvenir sellers would have gone to town. The crowds would be out, all right, with plenty of cheering. Imagine it locally, rather than at Westminster Abbey; Jesus comes to our town today, wishing to enter the place of worship. 'What are you doing in all your separate buildings, when I prayed that you might be one, so that the world might believe?' The equivalent of his overthrowing the tables of the money-changers might be an equally violent outburst. Would he challenge the lethargy of nominal Christians who turned up to cheer because he had come, but normally stay away; or would he find some hypocrisy in us, as though we were contented members of a happy worshipping club? There were outbursts of this kind by the prophets before Jesus (e.g. Isa. 1.10–20).

The message of Palm Sunday is not just a story from the past. These stories can be seen in their personal application also. Asking for Christmas again, that is to say asking for Christ to be born again in our hearts, holds few fears; we should not expect dramatic changes but a quiet transformation of our lives. But, as St Paul reminds us, we are the temple of God. Just as Jesus visited the temple in Jerusalem, so he can visit us, individually or corporately. As we prepare for our coming to Communion, we might try to envisage what would happen if Jesus were known to be entering the secret rooms of our thoughts, our hopes and fears and motives. Who would dare to say what Jesus might find and say, 'Take these things hence'? Or again, one sees pictures of Jesus as 'the unseen guest at every table, and the silent listener to every conversation'; that sort of thing can easily become sweet and sentimental if we are not careful. Do we really think Jesus would be too polite to criticize? If he told us he was more at home among the outcasts of society, would we be offended? Letting Christ into our lives, our homes, our church and society would have two sides. Palm Sunday was not all a matter of cheering and shouting, 'Hosanna to the Son of David.'

EASTER DAY

The initiative is with Christ

> Matthew 28.7 (AV) *'Behold, he goeth before you into Galilee; there shall ye see him.'*

Evidently the disciples had not fled from Jerusalem on the evening of Good Friday, however great their fear might have been. They stayed in Jerusalem, even though they locked their doors. Then in the bewildering events of Easter Day the message was given that Jesus was risen, that they should return to Galilee and that they would see him there. They did not go at once, and indeed they saw the risen Christ in the place where they were sheltering from the Jews in fear. Life must have seemed almost unreal and certainly utterly confusing. What on earth would happen next, and what were they to do? The response is now given – Go back to Galilee; you will see him there.

1 The risen Christ appeared in Galilee

Galilee was the scene of their ordinary life. Jerusalem had been the scene of the extra-ordinary. After living in the company of Jesus for the last two or three years, they could not return to normal without him, as though their discipleship had been but a dream. They had given up what had been normal to be with him; now they were to return, and he would be with them.

One thing is common to all the resurrection appearances; in

60

every case, the initiative was with Jesus. Whether they were fishing, having supper, walking to Emmaus, or going to look at the tomb, it was Jesus who came to them. If now they return to their homes, and as nearly as possible to ordinary life, he will come to them and be with them. It must have appeared almost past belief, but then the last two years had been full of things which they could not have imagined they would ever see or experience.

2 Look for the risen Christ in ordinary life

Today the same message comes to us. Jesus, of whom we read in the Gospels, is alive today. But if Jesus is alive, where shall we find him? We read about him, and have learned about him, in the Bible which is somehow different from ordinary books; we associate his presence with churches, and with services like Holy Communion, which are special places and special activities. These special things are not to be despised or ignored. But the same message comes to us as was given to the disciples. When you return home you will find that he has gone before you; you will find him there.

3 The prevenient Christ

In the Collect for today we pray that as by the special grace of God preventing, that is 'going before', us good desires are put into our minds, so by God's continual help we may put them to good effect. The living Lord Jesus is with us in our everyday life. He is wanting to lead us, to inspire us and to help us do his will; and through the abiding presence of the Holy Spirit, he does just that.

> And every virtue we possess
> And every victory won
> And every thought of holiness
> Are his alone.

The event of the first Easter Day, the resurrection of Jesus on the third day after the crucifixion, obviously is unique; it occurred on a particular day in a particular place. That Jesus lives is an abiding truth. He still goes before us, leading, inspiring and helping. May God help us all to realize his presence in our homes and daily life.

EASTERTIDE 1

The risen Lord

Luke 24.34 (AV) '*The Lord is risen indeed.*'

It is difficult for us, who live long after the event, to appreciate the dramatic effect of Easter. After all, we have known all the time that Lent was leading up to Holy Week and Good Friday and that the final climax would be Easter. It is unlikely that any of us can even remember being first told the Easter story. We have known all along that Jesus died on the cross, and that he rose again. This not only takes the element of surprise out of Easter but also dulls the sense of utter tragedy in respect of Good Friday.

1 The meaning of faith

Try to recapture how the disciples must have felt after Good Friday. Everything they had lived for had gone when Jesus had died. His death was more than the death of a friend, however close. They had given up, or been prepared to give up, everything to respond to his call; they had trusted him to the limit. Their action in following him was faith indeed. On Good Friday, the object and ground of their faith had died. Let us be quite clear; the disciples did not have faith in a cause of which

62

the leader happened to be Jesus, they had faith in Jesus and gradually learned from him what the object of his cause was. On Easter Day, the object of their faith, Jesus, their Master, was restored to them. Faith once again had meaning.

2 The meaning of hope

But their following of Jesus was more than an exercise of faith, it was a growing exercise of hope. Again let us be quite clear in our minds how little the disciples knew about Jesus when they first answered his call. A Confirmation candidate today knows far more about Jesus than the disciples did when they decided to follow him. The teaching in parables and the miracles, let alone the passion and resurrection, were yet to be experienced by the disciples. We can realize therefore how their initial faith must have seemed more and more justified, and how hope – in the sense of confident expectation that good things and good times lie ahead – must have grown in the disciples. I wonder sometimes whether such a growing hope is our experience as we go through life trying to trust in Jesus. But on Good Friday, all their hopes were shattered. On Easter Day every ground for their hope was restored.

3 The meaning of love

Then again it was not just faith and hope which died on Good Friday. They had been learning for three years the meaning of real love, which was embodied in Jesus. The cross was the climax of man's rejection of Jesus, with no retaliation or bitterness on his part. The subject of the devotion and loyalty of the disciples had been put to death. They were as bereaved as any person today losing their partner, or most intimate friend or relation. Then three days later, when the sense of loss was probably at its greatest, the miracle of the

resurrection transformed everything. Faith, hope and love had
died; faith, hope and love had been restored.

4 These three died and lived again

While Good Friday spelled the death of faith, hope and love
as far as the disciples were concerned, it was a showing of the
measure of God's faith and hope in man and his love for man.
God would not have allowed the cross to happen if he had not
loved man enough to want to save him. As a consequence,
Easter provides the sure ground for man's faith and hope in, and
love for, God. 'There are three things that last for ever: faith,
hope, and love' (NEB translation). Just as Christ died and rose
again, and is alive for ever; so these three died and lived again,
and abide for ever.

EASTERTIDE 2

A little while

John 16.16 (RV) *'A little while, and ye behold me no
more: and again a little while, and ye shall see me.'*

1 A difficult saying

No wonder the disciples were confused. It is easier for us, who
can look back on the record of the death and resurrection and
ascension of our Lord, to have some idea of what he meant. But
even to us it is a difficult saying. I have deliberately quoted from
the Revised Version which distinguishes the two different
words 'behold' and 'see'. We do not know, and there is no
means by which we can know, exactly what lies behind the
phrase, 'We have seen the Lord', which the disciples used with

such confidence after the resurrection. Part of the Easter message was that they must not cling to the past (e.g. John 20.17); part of the Ascension message is similar (e.g. Acts 1.11). Things had changed, and their relationship with Jesus was no longer that of physical learning and seeing. On the other hand, there was something in the relationship which death could not touch or destroy.

2 Sharing Christ's life

While the life, death and resurrection of Jesus were unique, there is a sense in which we can share in them. Obviously it is not sharing in any literal sense. But sayings such as 'Because I live, ye shall live also,' or 'He that believeth in me, though he were dead, yet shall he live; and whosoever liveth and believeth in me shall never die', point to a sharing in Christ's risen life in some way. The Bible brings out clearly and often that our hope of eternal life rests in our oneness with Christ. As in Adam (or unredeemed humanity) all die, even so in Christ shall all be made alive. Christ, risen from the dead, is become the first-fruits of them that sleep. But just as the mode of 'seeing' Christ before and after his resurrection was different, so it is with us; earthly means of communication and recognition are over.

3 Posted home

Death separates people and those who are 'left behind' feel a sense of emptiness and loneliness. I look back on a personal experience. In 1945, when the war came to an end, those of us who were serving in the Forces overseas had to wait our turn before being posted home. Relations at home were waiting just as anxiously as the men abroad. The posting notices went up at irregular intervals, and as each batch of servicemen left us there were Goodbyes at our end and, in due course, welcomes at the other end. While we were glad for their sake that they were going home, we missed them; they had become our friends, and we had to get used to living without them. In due course all that was forgotten when our own home-posting came through. In a very real sense, death is being 'posted home'. To be with Christ is to be where we belong. To a Christian, the prospect of death is far less alarming than the prospect of bereavement.

4 With Christ

Does the scripture give us any idea about what life after death will be like? Indeed it does. Above all, it is a life in Christ, and Christ's own teaching is that it begins now. Life, death and resurrection are not so much physical events in a time-sequence, but matters of relationship. Our resurrection life will be life eternally with Christ; if we love him, that will be heaven. Again, if the resurrection of Jesus is meant in any way to be a foretaste of our own resurrection, there will be some means of recognition and expression. If our life is hid with Christ, then that which is Christlike cannot die; either in us or in others. The things that spoil our earthly life – hunger and thirst, sorrow and parting, sin and pain – will be at an end; there will be a peace which passes all understanding.

The last words of Jesus to the disciples at the Ascension were, 'I am with you always (i.e. all day and every day) to the end of time.' He is equally with those no longer in the body. Neither life nor death can separate us from him. We do not cease to be members of the Body of Christ just because we happen to die.

> One family, we dwell in Him,
> One Church, above, beneath;
> Though now divided by the stream,
> The narrow stream of death.

The closer we are to Christ now the closer we are to those, no longer with us in the flesh, whose lives are hid with Christ in God.

66

ASCENSIONTIDE

The Sovereignty of Christ

'Thy kingdom come, thy will be done, on earth as it is in heaven.'

1 The counterpart of Christmas

'Now above the sky, he's King', we sing at Ascensiontide, and it all sounds so far off. All the picture-language used about heaven, particularly in the Book of Revelation, sounds very unearthly, perhaps deliberately. It seems very much as if 'between us and you there is a great gulf fixed.' In some ways the Ascension is the counterpart of Christmas. At Christmas 'he came down to earth from heaven, who is God and Lord of all'; at Ascensiontide, he returned from earth to heaven, and took our manhood with him. But if we think that the gap was only breached for thirty years or so, we are very wrong. However we may understand the phrase that he sits at the right hand of God in the glory of the Father, his own promise is that he is with us all the time and always will be.

2 King for us

The sovereignty of Christ is very much part of the message of the Ascension, but that sovereignty does not just exist in some far-off realm above the sky. The kingdom of God is, or can be, within us and among us. Wherever Christ's will is done, wherever he is acknowledged as supreme, there is his kingdom. Many of the marks of his kingdom are described in the parables, and the sermon on the mount gives a picture of the kind of behaviour that may be expected of any person who acknowledges Christ's right to rule his life. When we see that kind of behaviour prompted by unconditional love, we have a brief glimpse of the kingdom of heaven; at that moment and in that place, the petition in the Lord's Prayer, 'thy kingdom come – on earth as it is in heaven', has come true.

3 King by right

Jesus Christ is King by right, whether we acknowledge his sovereignty or not. The psalmist recognized this of God, long ago. 'The Lord is King, be the people never so impatient: he sitteth between the cherubim, be the earth never so unquiet' (Ps. 99.1). When Christ's kingdom comes on earth in its fulness, it will be seen not only in the structures of society but in the hearts of men. Many people today, including statesmen of various nations and scientists and doctors and policemen and others, are working for Christ's kingdom without consciously realizing the fact. To establish and to maintain peace, to work for just and fair conditions in industry, to seek to bring healing to the sick and aid to the handicapped and under privileged, all these are forwarding the kingdom. At the personal level, also, when we allow Christ to take control of our wills and try to do and to say what we believe he would do or say, his kingdom comes both in the circumstance and in our hearts.

4 The first fruit of the Ascension

In both spheres, that is to say in the affairs of society and in the hearts of individuals, it is the Holy Spirit who is at work. Jesus said, 'He will take of mine and will show it unto you.' The ability to see things and people as Jesus sees them is a gift of the Spirit; the power to turn that vision into action is also a gift of the Spirit. We need the gift of the Spirit both to think and to do those things that are right. The gift of the Spirit, for which we especially thank God at Whitsuntide, is the firstfruit of the Ascension.

Yes, Christ Jesus is King by right; and he sends the Holy Spirit in answer to the prayer 'Thy kingdom come, thy will be done, on earth as it is in heaven.'

PENTECOST

The Spirit of truth

John 16.13 (AV) '*When he, the Spirit of truth, is come, he will guide you into all truth.*'

The Collect for today prays that we may have a right judgement in all things, through the guidance of the Holy Spirit. What is clear from the teaching of Jesus is that no one knows all there is to know about God and his will; there is always more truth to learn, and always the need for divine guidance in men's actions. The encouraging message of this festival of Whitsuntide is that God the Holy Spirit helps us in both these things.

1 Truth beyond explanation

In the matter of truth, the Creeds of the Christian Church – arrived at after years of discussion and prayer – point the way to truth, and turn us away from many falsehoods. But they do not, indeed they cannot, express the whole truth. To take a rather simple example, we say that we believe in 'the resurrection of the dead'; but who can say exactly what that means? It points us away from the error of thinking that this life is everything. It warns us, perhaps, that there will be judgement; it raises the hope that earthly love and friendship have an eternal dimension. In a way beyond our understanding, our own resurrection depends upon the resurrection of Jesus

Christ. 'As in Adam all die, even so in Christ shall all be made alive.' But the resurrection of Christ, one of the events in history on which our faith depends, is a mystery; words may proclaim it, they cannot explain it.

2 Truth beyond words

Of all the seasons of the Christian year, that of Whitsuntide shows up most clearly the limitations of human language to express divine truth. This applies on many human levels also. The look in the bridegroom's eye and the smile on the bride's face as they exchange their vows say much more than is contained in their promises. Love cannot be expressed in words alone; love is spiritual, love is of God. So too the truth of Whitsuntide is beyond words, in every sense of that phrase. If you are one of those people who say, 'I can understand what happened at Christmas, and on Good Friday and Easter, but Whitsuntide is beyond me', that is good. Whitsuntide will always be beyond us, but if we are facing the right way 'looking unto Jesus' then the Holy Spirit will be with us to strengthen, enlighten, guide and encourage us.

3 Truth in Jesus Christ

The event in the life of every communicant which we associate with the gift of the Holy Spirit is Confirmation. Before the day comes, there has been quite an extended period of preparation and instruction. Even if a candidate were to think he knows all he needs to know, the parish priest knows otherwise. (A similar remark could be made about Ordination, when the gift of the Holy Spirit is invoked; but that's another story!) Confirmation is the beginning of a new stage in one's pilgrimage with Christ, not a 'passing-out' ceremony. Christian knowledge is that of a person, not of a collection of facts. We can learn the facts through instruction and from books, but knowledge of the person of Christ is spiritually given. Jesus speaks of the Spirit leading us into all truth; he also said, 'I am the truth.' We grow in our knowledge of him, as we do of our earthly friends, by constant contact with him in prayer and by association with others who are trying to live close to him. It is a humbling thought, but it is true that other people will derive some of their knowledge of Jesus from us if we are known and seen to be living close to him. All this is part of the work of the Spirit of truth, for which we thank God today.

PENTECOST 1

TRINITY SUNDAY

The Trinity

> Revelation 4.8 (AV) *'Holy, holy, holy, Lord God Almighty, which was, and is, and is to come.'*

This Sunday has traditionally marked the half-way stage in the Christian year. From Advent, through Christmas, Epiphany, Lent, Holy Week and Easter, and the Sundays up to Whitsunday we have been reminded of the acts of God for the redemption of mankind. We have been encouraged to think about our Christian faith. In the weeks that follow, till Advent comes round again, we are encouraged to think of our Christian life. Putting it over-simply, the first half concentrates on doctrine and the second half on duty. This particular Sunday dwells on what is probably the most difficult doctrine of all, that of the Trinity. The late Professor Charles Raven used to say, 'If you think you understand the Trinity, you've got him wrong.'

1 The ground for our life

The complicated Athanasion Creed, which used to be found under the odd title, 'At Morning Prayer', in the 1662 Prayer Book, opens with one simple and profound truth. 'The Catholic faith is this; that we worship one God in Trinity.' In so many words, the faith of the Church is not that we understand God, but that we worship him. There is all the difference in the world. The right response of man to God, of creature to creator, is that of worship.

> Rejoice! The Lord is King!
> Your Lord and King adore;
> Mortals, give thanks and sing,
> And triumph evermore:
> Lift up your heart, lift up your voice;
> Rejoice, again I say, rejoice.

Joy, thanksgiving, adoration and praise are — or should be — the first-fruits of our belief in the sovereignty of God. Those unattached, nominal, Christians who say that it is not the Christian faith that matters but living the Christian life do not realize what the Christian life involves. It is a lot more than being kind to others. The command to love one's neighbour as oneself is very pre-Christian; Christ's commandment is that we love one another *as he has loved us*. That commandment cannot be understood, let alone obeyed, unless we are 'looking unto Jesus'.

2 The example for our life

The Christian life is the consequence of the Christian faith, and faith in God as Trinity provides three aspects of that life. If God, all-holy and all-good, is the Creator of all things and Father of all mankind, our duty to him is that of obedience; our duty to our neighbour is that of brotherly love within the family of God. The fatherhood of God provides the ground and

72

the context of our way of life. Our faith in Jesus, as God incarnate, provides the model for our way of life. To become Christlike is the highest human goal, for Jesus is man as God would have him be. When Jesus taught that we should be perfect as our Father in heaven is perfect (Matt. 5.48), he summed up the teaching of the sermon on the mount in one sentence. But unless we knew what that perfection would look like in human terms, his teaching would have little or no meaning. Fortunately we see that perfection in its fulness in Jesus.

3 The strength for our life

But as soon as we set our hearts and minds on the imitation of Jesus, we find that it is quite beyond our own unaided strength. To go on forgiving again and again, seventy times seven, is more than we can face. To be generous to the unthankful, not to be anxious about earthly things, to love our enemies, these are counsels of perfection to mere mortals. This is where our faith in God, the Holy Spirit, comes into its own. We are not mere mortals left on our own to copy an impossibly high example or pursue an impossibly high ideal. God gives us a strength which is divine to help us live the Christian life. We do not need to understand the eternal relationship of the Holy Spirit with the other persons in the Godhead, but we do need to call on the guidance and strength of the Holy Spirit for our daily living.

So then our faith in God as Trinity, Father, Son and Holy Spirit provides the ground, the example and the strength for our Christian life here and now.

Doubt

Mark 9.24 (AV) *'Lord, I believe; help thou my unbelief.'*

1 A little faith

The fact that the father of the boy with the dumb spirit brought him to Jesus at all is some evidence of his faith. At the lowest level, at least it was worth a try. There would have been enough stories going round about healings done by Jesus to make a man with a son like that wonder whether he could do anything for him; there was nothing to lose. Clearly he was really anxious about the lad, not selfishly for his own sake but genuinely for the lad's sake. He had already been in touch with some of the disciples, but they had not been successful in their attempts to help (verse 18). One can imagine the effect of that failure on the confidence of the father; it certainly helps us to understand the request, 'If thou canst do anything. . . .' Then he had to face the challenge, 'All things are possible to him that believeth.' Did he believe that? Do we?

2 Faith and doubt mixed

I suppose there are a certain number of sincere scientific humanists who genuinely do not believe in any supernatural power. Equally, there are a few people who would believe anything. In between lies the majority, which probably includes all of us, who say we believe (and believe what we say) but have varying degrees of doubt. Sometimes prayers seem to be answered in the way we think right, and we are full of faith. Sometimes we pray hard for something that seems so right, and it does not happen and we begin to doubt the value of prayer altogether; if there is such a thing as divine providence, it seems quite inscrutable.

If this worries us, that is good. Most preachers know something of the tension between speaking confidently about the power of God and his willingness to answer prayer and at the same time knowing that it does not always seem to happen as we would wish. If the preacher begins to ask himself, 'Am I a hypocrite?' at least he is being honest. If he can convince himself that he is not a hypocrite, well and good; his faith is real but weak. If he cannot so convince himself, he really has a problem. But most people do not have to face that crisis so obviously; outwardly they profess faith in the providence of God, inwardly they are full of doubts.

3 Doubt concealed by habit

It is not only about the providence of God that they have doubts. Do they really believe in the Resurrection of Jesus? The stories about it are very confusing. Do they really believe in the turning of water into wine at Cana in Galilee, and does it matter all that much? I have been saying 'Do they believe?' Perhaps I should say, 'Do we believe?' I am thinking of people like ourselves who still come to church and still say our prayers. It is easy to avoid the anxiety of the father of the boy with the dumb spirit by putting an iron curtain between our outward profession of faith and our inner agnosticism. Our prayers and our religious habits are just habits; good habits, yes, and probably pleasing ones too, but habits none the less. We inculcate these habits in our children and hope they will not ask too persistently, 'Does God really listen to our prayers and answer them? If so, why did Grandma die instead of getting better?'

4 Honest doubt

Honest doubt is better than that. Honest doubt admits the

weakness of faith, but at least the weak faith is real and we are concerned that it is not stronger. The response of the father, 'Lord I believe; help thou my weakness of faith,' is one which we should constantly be making. The answer to that prayer will probably not be a sensational miracle, but rather an opening of our eyes to many less dramatic examples of God's activity in the world and in our lives.

EVERYDAY FAILINGS 2

Pretence

> James 1.22 (AV) *'Be ye doers of the word, and not hearers only, deceiving your own selves.'*

1 Colour prejudice

The number of warnings against pretence and sham in the Bible is enormous. There are false prophets who cry 'Peace, Peace' where there is no peace; there were those prophets who said, 'Sword and famine shall not be in this land' (Jer. 14.15) of whom God said he did not send them. Is this so terribly out of date? When we read of wars and riots, of religious persecution in far-off lands, have we never thought or said, 'That would never happen here'? It is easy to shut our eyes to reality and pretend that things are other than what they are in fact. If we say there is no colour prejudice in England, if we believe that sort of thing happens only in Southern Africa, we deceive ourselves. We are shutting our eyes to the facts. But, if you were a Christian in a land where there was colour segregation, how would you behave? It is one thing to protest that laws are wrong, it is another thing to behave as though such laws do not exist. Our Christian brothers and sisters in South Africa need our prayers that they may inspire public opinion rather than outrage it.

But there are so many other ways of deceiving ourselves. Some are quite harmless, like pretending we are younger – or older – than we really are; if we try hard enough we manage to deceive ourselves, but are less likely to deceive others. But there are some forms of self-deception which are common today and hinder God's plan.

One is the widespread opinion that the laws of God are only good advice. Some of them, after all, are very old; they may have been applicable a thousand years before Christ, but things are different now. The fact that this may be true of the ritual laws can delude us into thinking that it is true of all. The logical consequence is to regard sin as a bad habit which would be better given up, rather than an offence against God which needs forgiveness. If we say that we have no sin, we deceive ourselves. There is a God who has a will for men, and that will has been expressed in the moral laws enshrined in the Bible. The ten Commandments have not yet been repealed. But it is not only the ten Commandments that we think are out of date. Is the sermon on the mount an impossible ideal? 'Let's pretend that Jesus didn't mean what he said about marriage and divorce' is a not uncommon attitude today. Or again let's pretend that pre-marital chastity was no more than a wise precaution before the days of contraception.

3 Christian unity

In a quite different field, that of Christian unity, it is easy to deceive ourselves by pretending things are different from what they really are. The speed with which the situation has changed over the last twenty-five years makes this easier. On the one hand, we may not appreciate the great changes that have taken place either in our own Communion or in other Churches; we deceive ourselves into thinking that things are as they were, and will never change. This leads to the sinful acceptance of

77

division. 'What does it matter, anyway? If "they" like to do things their way, who are we to interfere'? Alternatively there can be the pretence that the divisions are more apparent than real and that there is such a basic unity that the differences are of little consequence. 'If we say that we have no sin,' by thinking these things do not matter, 'we deceive ourselves and the truth is not in us'. On the personal level, it is easy to deceive ourselves either by thinking that church membership does not really matter or, quite the reverse, that because we are conscientious church members all is well. 'Be ye doers of the word and not hearers only, deceiving your own selves.'

EVERYDAY FAILINGS 3

Pride

> John 13.3–4 (TEV) *'Jesus knew that the Father had given him complete power; he knew that he had come from God and was going to God. So he rose from the table, took off his outer garment and tied a towel round his waist.'*

1 Jesus abjured pride

The washing of the feet of the disciples by Jesus is the most familiar of the examples of his humility. St John makes it clear that Jesus wanted it to be remembered in this way; 'I have set an example for you, so that you will do just what I have done for you.' Greatness is shown in humility, nobility is shown in service. This corresponds with his teaching after the mother of James and John had asked that a special place should be reserved for them in his kingdom. 'You know that the rulers of the heathen have power over them, and the leaders have complete authority. This, however, is not the way it should be among you. If one of you wants to be great, he must be the servant of the rest' (Matt. 20, 25–26 (TEV)).

2 Pride is objectionable

All this is very familiar. There are few faults in other people more obvious or more objectionable than pride. Indeed there is often a delightful pleasure in seeing a proud person brought down a peg. A story is told of a proud organist, in the days when organs were pumped by hand, who was profusely thanked after a recital. He sat down to play an encore and in the middle of it, all went quiet. He cursed the organ-blower loudly, but the latter quietly said, 'You can't play this organ unless someone helps you, by blowing it for you.'

3 Spiritual pride

But while we despise pride when we see it, and know that we are called to be humble, it is quite easy to be proud of our humility. Evelyn Underhill warns us of the spiritual danger of constantly going into the greenhouse of the soul to see how our humility is getting on. In the last resort, humility is a quite unconscious virtue. It is not the quality of the slave who looks down and is made to feel small and unworthy; it is the quality of the child who looks up in wonder and trust. 'When I consider the heavens, the works of thy fingers, the moon and the stars which thou hast ordained, what is man that thou art mindful of him?' The concern of God for mankind is indeed occasion for wonder, and that concern is revealed in its fulness in the coming of Christ. The Psalmist wrote 'Lift up your heads O ye gates, and be ye lift up ye everlasting doors, and the king of glory shall come in.' But how silent was his coming. The birth of the Babe of Bethlehem is the measure of the humility of God. Being in the form of God, he emptied himself and took upon him the form of a servant, and (even) as a man, he humbled himself and was obedient unto death. He did not humble himself in spite of his divinity; rather, he revealed his divinity by his humility.

Humility is consideration for others, without measurement of merit and without thought of reward. When a patient arrives in hospital needing urgent treatment, his morals and rank are irrelevant. There is a basic equality at the earthly level of our being. There is a divine equality at the highest level of our being also. Peasant and king, black and white, share the same preliminaries of birth and also the same redemption from sin and the same hope of eternal life. Tubby Clayton put over the door of Toc. H in Poperinghe during the first World War, 'All rank abandon, ye who enter here'. Comparing ourselves with others may lead to pride and scorn, or to envy and shame; it will not lead to humility. The secret is rather to have the mind of Christ, to treat each neighbour whom we meet as the most important person in the world at that moment, and so to grow into the likeness of Christ.

EVERYDAY FAILINGS 4

Envy

> Matthew 20.12 (AV) '*These last have wrought but one hour, and thou hast made them equal unto us which have borne the burden and heat of the day.*'

1 Examples of envy

The reaction of those who had laboured all day was very reasonable, and pity any man who would try to use this parable as a basis for Trade Union negotiations. It was not told for that sort of reason, but to give a picture of envy on the one hand and the generosity of God on the other. Envy is not the same thing as jealousy. Jealousy in the scriptures is a passion to protect something that belongs to you; thus God is jealous for his people, and also for his own honour. (See Josh. 24.19; Exod. 20.5). Envy is being angry because someone else has some good fortune; it does not necessarily mean that we want to exchange places, but we begrudge them their good fortune. Biblical examples are numerous. While we are not given the reason why Abel's offering was accepted and Cain's refused, Cain showed typical signs of envy; 'Cain was very wroth and his countenance fell.' We see the same symptoms between Jacob and Esau, Saul and David, Rachel and Leah and others. Perhaps the parable of the prodigal son brings it out most clearly, the elder brother was angry because of the welcome given to his brother. The father does his utmost to persuade him to come in, but he will not; he tells his father that his brother is a rotter and does not deserve this treatment. Let us face it, the elder brother was right; the young lad did not *deserve* this treatment, he was *given* it. It was not a reward for coming home, it was overflowing love expressing itself.

2 Envy leads to anger

In all these stories we are spectators, looking at the situation from outside, and recognizing all the symptoms of envy in other people. Sooner or later the spirit of the Lord will say to us, as Nathan said to David, 'Thou art the man' (2 Sam. 12.7); yet once we realize we may be involved, it is surprising how distorted our vision can be. Envy, we say to ourselves, is a form of inner protest against injustice, and are we not right to be angry at injustice? If we hear of a child being punished for what someone else has done, or an old woman overcharged because she cannot read the price on a label, we are right to be angry. Envy is a kind of protest against someone having some *good* fortune that they do not deserve. It is not complaining that we did not win a prize; if the winner was better and deserved to win, we may be disappointed but that is not envy. Why should Leah have child after child, but Rachel (whom Jacob really did love) was childless for so many years? Or to come nearer home, Tommy is two, and his mother goes away for a few days to give birth to Mary. Now a lot of the attention that used to be given to Tommy has to be given to Mary; visitors and strangers in the street ignore Tommy and go into raptures about the new arrival. What on earth has Mary done to deserve all this? Only too easily, envy can creep in and breed anger, if not hatred, and sow the seeds of a divided family.

3 Envy leads to rebellion against God

In the last resort, however, envy becomes anger with God, because he does give more generously than justice would demand. It is the counterpart of scorn, which disdains those who do not have certain elements of good fortune. Scorn quickly leads to pride and to hardness of heart; envy quickly leads to rebellion against God for not being just and giving to those who do not deserve. Seen in this light, envy takes us to the heart of the Gospel, for it is a protest against the love and generosity of God, revealed in Jesus Christ. In our hearts of hearts, we would like to be able to earn our salvation; if we cannot do it by good works, at least it can be conditional on the orthodoxy of our belief or even the genuineness of our penitence. But the offer of the love of God is not conditional upon anything; it was while we were yet sinners that Christ died for us, not on condition we repented.

4 The remedy for envy

Where, then, is the remedy for envy to be found? Let us face the fact, only by the grace of God. He wants us to rejoice with those who do rejoice, to be glad at his generosity which results in the good fortune of others. In the General Thanksgiving we 'give thee most hearty thanks for all thy goodness . . . to us and to all men'. Of course we must thank God for his goodness to us, not that we are not as other men; real gratitude will make us realize that we do not deserve our good fortune. Thanking God for his goodness to others will gradually drive envy out of our hearts, and make room for rejoicing instead.

EVERYDAY FAILINGS 5

False modesty

> Matthew 5.16 (AV) *'Let your light so shine before men that they may see your good works, and glorify your father which is in heaven.'*
> Matthew 6.1 (AV) *'Take heed that ye do not your alms before men, to be seen of them; otherwise ye have no reward of your Father which is in heaven.'*

1 An apparent contradiction

At first sight these two sayings of our Lord, both from the sermon on the mount, sound contradictory. What is more, there is no obvious half way house between them. To take an example, suppose there is a public appeal for some very deserving charity, and a prominent local person agrees to make a substantial donation. The appeal organizer wants to give this publicity to encourage other givers; the donor insists otherwise. Is it obvious which is right? Even an envelope scheme for church collections can hide both generosity and any lack of it.

2 The extremes are wrong

Of these two sayings of Jesus, the one which tells us to do things secretly is the more congenial to most of us. We dislike people who boast, and a child who tries to show off at school is in for a hard time. Often the attempt to show off is a compensation for some other weakness which we want to hide. Clearly we can take either boasting or reticence to extremes. Jesus plainly condemns boasting; when our 'good works' are seen, it is to be in such a way that the glory is ascribed to God, not to us. When a ship sees the beam from a lighthouse, and so can confirm its position, the captain does not praise the lighthouse keeper; but he is grateful all the same. When in traffic after dark, you do not praise drivers who have their lights on; indeed you would be very cross if they didn't. Let those lights so shine that others may drive more safely. Lights are meant to be seen.

3 Feelings need to be expressed

In much the same way, our feelings (if good) need to be expressed. Just about the first words a child learns after Mum and Dad, are Please and Thank you. Gratitude needs to be expressed, to your neighbour and to God. Praise and pleasure need to be expressed. If someone has done a job well, say so. An ounce of praise is worth a ton of criticism. Clearly it needs to be genuine and not fulsome; a ton of praise is probably worth less than an ounce. When a young man, or a young lady for that matter, is in love he wants to do something or to say something to express it. Love needs expression as a plant needs light, both to grow and to be seen; obviously for less intimate friends, such expressions are probably confined to birthdays and Christmas. What we express to others, we should apply also to God. If we are aware of our blessings, we should thank God for them. If we are worried about something which has gone wrong, in our own lives or in the world at large, we should say so to God in our prayers. Indeed the more sincerely we thank God for his goodness or pray that his will be done, the more our gratitude and our concern will grow.

Unexpressed feelings soon fade and die. We read an article, or an appeal, for a highly deserving cause and say to ourselves,

'They're doing good work, they are.' But if we do nothing, by way of prayer or gift, our approval is very shallow and shortlived. If, however, we do express our feelings by a gift, we are doing just what our Lord asked. The cause is helped to grow and its good work will be seen; others will not praise us for supporting it, but have more reason to praise God for the work that is being done. If we say we are concerned about the spread of the gospel or the plight of refugees, the loneliness of old people or the care of unwanted children, we must show it. If we show it corporately as a church, the glory will be to God.

EVERYDAY DUTIES 1

Fear and love of God

> Deuteronomy 6.5 (AV) *'The fear of the Lord is the beginning of wisdom.'*
> Proverbs 9.10 (AV) *'Thou shalt love the Lord thy God.'*

1 First fears

There is a well-known prayer (Collect for Trinity 2 in BCP) in which we pray that we may have a perpetual fear and love of God's holy name. But how can fear and love be combined? Does not fear show itself by shrinking away from and trying to avoid the object of fear? Love, on the other hand, seeks to get nearer to its object, to find and to grasp, to have and to hold. If we think of those things of which we are afraid, we might turn to our first fears. Perhaps the fear of the dark is the first, and most parents will leave some light burning, however dim, so that their children will not be afraid at night. The dark is the unknown. In the same way some people are afraid of lightning, which is powerful but unpredictable. Fear of wild beasts, fear of the enemy in war, fear of storms at sea, all share the idea of the unpredictable and overpowering.

2 Fear as awe

This is not the sense in which the fear of the Lord is used. Rather, it refers to a sense of awe, of mystery and of wonder. We are not on equal terms with God; he is creator, we are created; we are mortal, he is immortal. 'I am weak but thou art mighty, Hold me with thy powerful hand', is one of the better expressions of this sense. Again, 'The waves of the sea are mighty and rage horribly, but yet the Lord who dwelleth on high is mightier.' The fear of the Lord is the recognition, not only of his power and might, but of his 'otherness'. There is a sense of awe, not a sense of being frightened; indeed the very power of God is part of the assurance that we need not be afraid.

3 Love as the will to please

But if the fear of the Lord is both understandable and natural when seen in this way, the command to love God sounds strange. Love seeks the company of its object, and if we are not afraid of God it is right that we should want to be in his company. Can we love to order, however? Love must be freely given. We seek the company of someone because we enjoy their company, and that is not something which can be commanded. Clearly the word love has a richer meaning also, and implies the will to do what pleases God. In respect of our human neighbours it implies not so much doing what would please them, but rather what is for their greatest good. A mother's love may give pleasure to her child most of the time, but occasionally may mean saying 'No.'

4 Love and fear combined

Perhaps on the human level the conjunction of love and fear is seen best in the marriage promise which is both to love and honour. (Note that each partner is not asked, 'Do you love . . .?', but 'Will you love . . .?') In one sense, marriage is the legal union of two separate persons; they become Mr and Mrs So-and-So. In the years that follow, this unity is progressively expressed and deepened. But honour is the recognition of the 'otherness' of our partner, a recognition which is vital to a happy marriage; however long the marriage, the sense of otherness remains.

In the Lord's Prayer these two thoughts are both given expression. 'Hallowed be thy name' embodies the thought of awe and reverence towards our Father, who is in heaven. 'Thy will be done' is a prayer of love, our desire to do on earth what will please God. He is constantly showing his love for us by seeking our greatest good; our love is a response. We love, because he first loved us. Lifted in this way, fear and love express our richest attitude both to God and to our neighbour.

EVERYDAY DUTIES 2

Caution and courage

> Matthew 10.16 (AV) *'Behold, I send you forth as sheep in the midst of wolves: be ye therefore wise as serpents, and harmless as doves.'*

1 Toleration

It is quite a long time since there was any organized religious persecution in this country. There are, of course, small groups like the Moonies which some people feel ought to be outlawed; but what the Americans call the 'main-line Churches' are very tolerant of one another. Perhaps we should be a bit more thankful that we did not live in the sixteenth century; but perhaps we are not so fixed in our opinions that we should run any risk of being burned at the stake. We expect to be tolerated and in our turn we will tolerate people of other persuasions; we won't bother them, so long as they don't bother us. We are as harmless as doves; our going to church doesn't hurt anybody, and we are reasonably in love and charity with our neighbours.

2 Persecution

Why, then, have Christians been persecuted in the past? From the first Christian martyr, St Stephen, we read of persecution of Christians by the Jews. When you come to think of it, the proclamation, 'Jesus of Nazareth, a man approved of God . . . ye have taken, and by wicked hands have crucified and slain; God hath raised up', would scarcely have seemed harmless to the Jews at the time. Saul of Tarsus certainly thought that Christians should not be tolerated and, when he himself became a Christian, did not expect to be tolerated. The Romans had problems with the Christians who refused to worship Caesar and so were regarded as disloyal. Others felt that the Christians should be outlawed as a secret society. Right up to modern times dictators and Christians have been at variance because the Church deemed that the dictators were claiming more authority than God has given to man. But it has not only been non-Christian or secular power which has done the persecuting. Inter-Church enmity backed, it may be, by secular power has expressed itself in burnings at the stake even in this country.

Today most of us would agree with the town clerk of Ephesus (Acts 19) when he appealed to the people to calm down; these Christians are harmless and protest will not do anybody any good. Perhaps we feel the same about anti-nuclear demonstrations, or even anti-papal ones recently; ignore them as far as possible, and they will do no harm. Is this what Jesus meant by being harmless as doves? Perhaps we should note that the context in which that remark is placed in the gospel is a warning that his followers must expect persecution for their loyalty to him.

3 Complacency

Is our faith really meant to be revolutionary? If so, does our practice of it proclaim its meaning? Indeed, is that entirely our fault? Living here in Britain where the Church is officially recognized, where (since the Catholic Emancipation Act just over a hundred and fifty years ago) there is virtually no official religious intolerance, it is too easy to be complacent. If we want to go to church, nobody will stop us; if we do not, nobody can make us. Belonging to the Church does not cost us so much in the matter of money that our standard of living is in danger. Compared with the amount spent on drink and tobacco, or on armaments, the amount given by English Christians to the work of the Church is negligible. Being a Christian in England today is so easy, and so undemanding, that the Church is more likely to lose ground by decay through lack of self-sacrifice and discipline, than by persecution. We are as harmless as doves, but not as wise as serpents. The accusation against the church in Laodicea (Rev. 3.16) was that it was lukewarm, not cold enough to cause any offence and not warm enough to cut any ice. Our task is to discern what difference in our home life and in society the real sovereignty of God would make and, with all the wisdom at our command, to work to that end. If we suffer as a result, God will sustain us. But whether we get taken seriously by the world, for good or ill, God's kingdom will come. Even if we were left out, God will triumph.

Personal responsibility

> Ezekiel 18.2–3 *'The fathers have eaten sour grapes, and the children's teeth are on edge. As I live, saith the Lord God, ye shall no longer have occasion to use this proverb.'*

1 Home influence

In fact, variations of this proverb are common. One hears of villages so interrelated that if one person is bitten everybody scratches; I once heard of a family which was said to be so united that if you stroked the dog, the cat purred. Something of the truth of the proverb is to be found in the second of the ten Commandments. It sounds so unfair but however much we may protest, there is a large element of truth there. Illegitimate children, and those with fathers in prison, suffer greatly for their parents' faults. Family solidarity is such that children get their standards from their parents, standards of honesty and relations to neighbours in particular. Every juvenile court magistrate knows this only too well. There is a story told of a very new prison chaplain who went to see the governor. 'I've just had a long talk with So-and-So; he has a very disturbed home background.' 'You're quite right,' replied the Governor, 'but let me tell you about the other 597 inmates'.

2 Personal responsibility

Somehow or other two truths have to be combined. Parental influence and example is great, but it does not excuse the behaviour of the children; we each have to accept responsibility for our own actions. On the one hand, we cannot demand respect because we come from a good family: on the other hand, we cannot disclaim responsibility by blaming our parents. Husbands cannot salve their conscience about the worship of God because their wives go to church or because their children attend Sunday School. Each man must work out his own salvation. Membership of the Church is indeed important, but of itself it will not save us. That would be an echo of the saying, 'We have Abraham for our father.' Jewish solidarity was very strong; to Abraham and his seed were the promises made.

3 Individual faith

Ezekiel, and Jeremiah also (Chapter 31), is stressing the truth of personal responsibility. No man can save his brother. In our Christian faith this truth is paramount. Christ has died for the sins of the whole world, but it rests with each of us individually to accept his sacrifice for ourselves. The faith of the Church must become our faith; each of us must turn to Christ – which is what is meant by personal conversion. Part of the protest of the Reformers against prayers for the dead was related to the thought of personal judgement. At the judgement seat no third party can save us, only Christ himself. It will not avail at the last judgement to say 'Did we not prophesy in thy name . . . and in thy name do many mighty works?' (Matt. 7.22). Did we not support the church functions and do this and that? Indeed the impenitent thief might even say, 'Did I not hang on a cross with you on that fateful Friday?'

4 Influence

But the other truth has a positive side. We can and do influence others for good. We rejoice to hear of the dramatic conversion of the complete outsider, but the influence of believing parents and of Christian teachers at school must have enabled millions of children to hear the good news and to want to respond. While it may be true that many prisoners have a disturbed home background, how very many more are not inside largely because of the influence of their family. We are bound together by kinship and by love, thank God, and we would not have it otherwise. This means that the social behaviour of those of us who claim to be Christians will influence not only our families but many whom we scarcely know at all. Others will, to some extent, judge the faith we say we hold by our way of living and we may be wholly unaware of it.

These two truths remain. The sins of the fathers are, in this world, visited on their children; as a result we have a responsibility towards others. But we have a personal responsibility towards God for our own way of life, and our acceptance of salvation by Christ must be equally personal.

EVERYDAY DUTIES 4

Loyalty to God and country

> Matthew 22.21 (AV) *'Render unto Caesar the things which are Caesar's; and unto God the things that are God's.'*

1 Different loyalties

It is good that we should pray regularly for those who have responsibility for government, not just in our own country but in the whole world. If we have a double loyalty (as expressed in the promise of a Boy Scout or Girl Guide) this is only right and proper. For most of us most of the time, this double loyalty presents little problem. We have other loyalties also, such as our family, our particular part of the Church and perhaps some society to which we belong. The Old Testament law distinguished three loyalties: to God, to one's family and to one's neighbour. These are expressed in the first four, the fifth, and the last five of the ten Commandments; if kept in that order, there should not be an conflict of loyalties. The teaching of Jesus would seem to imply that in fulfilling one loyalty, you are fulfilling the others. By healing a sick man on the Sabbath, one is not dishonouring God.

2 Conflict of loyalties

It is, of course, easy to pervert that idea. By mowing the lawn on a Sunday, a man may be helping his wife; but it does not excuse him from his duty to worship God. At a more serious level, however, real conflict may arise. A man or woman has a loyalty to a trade union, to his family and to the public. If a strike is called with which he does not agree, where does his loyalty lie? Quite apart from the effect on family income, this kind of situation can pose real problems. Nurses and others in the caring professions feel this deeply; but in a strike of, say, grave-diggers or train drivers, it is by no means easy to measure the hurt caused to others.

3 Action on Christian principles

In a truly Christian community, in which selfish interest gives way to concern for others and is balanced by the concern of others for oneself, these conflicts should not arise. A Christian community is far more than a community of Christians. It is rather a community in which all public decisions are based on Christian principles, in which justice and mercy are combined, in which there is opportunity for all to share God's gifts and in which personal licence is restrained in such a way that the freedom of one does not restrict the freedom of others. It is not enough that Parliament should open with prayer, but that all its members should acknowledge that the pattern of the kingdom of God provides the principles on which the laws of the land should rest. To take a particular example: a school is not a Christian school just because it opens the day with prayer, or even because all its members belong to a church. Rather if it is, even unconsciously, recognized that all knowledge relates to God's world, that the growth of character should be into the likeness of Christ, and that its common life should recognize the infinite worth of each of its members and that each puts the welfare of others before self-interest. Such a school may well contain pupils and staff of other faiths and other races than white. Obviously the more genuine Christians there are in any community, be it a school, or trade union, or the country as a whole, the easier it will be for it to act as a Christian society, to think in Christian categories and to act on Christian principles.

4 Prayer for our country

How does a prayer for our country and its rulers affect us, and how can we help it to be answered? First, by ourselves acknowledging our personal loyalty to God, shown by our worship – putting God first – and our acceptance of his sovereignty over our own lives. Then again, even if the most we can do is to exercise our voting power in a Christian way, to use any influence we have in society; this would include making our homes an example of Christian family life, and going about our work in a Christian way. But there is a particular responsibility for the Church as a community of Christians to set an example and lead the way in matters of social concern. The work of the Churches through Christian Aid in its care for refugees and those in distress in the Third World is one example. But nearer home, it is one thing to criticize countries where there is racial discrimination, but quite another for the Church to work for racial harmony in our own cities. In many such ways the Church can influence public opinion and behaviour.

For the Christian there are two loyalties, to God and country. Let part of our prayer be that our country may be so ordered and governed that these two loyalties may not conflict.

EVERYDAY DUTIES 5

Remembering and forgetting

Luke 16.25 (JB) *'My son, remember that during your life good things came your way.'*

1 Thanksgiving for memory

If we were to compile a list of those gifts of God for which we had cause to be specially thankful, I wonder how many of us would include the gift of memory. Imagine what life would be like without it. We should have to start every friendship again from scratch; all the joys of the past would be lost to us wholly and, admittedly, all the sorrows as well. We should live, rather like butterflies, entirely in the present. Like a straw on a flowing stream, we should be carried along the tide of time and in due course be plunged into the abyss of oblivion. But thank God we have the gift of memory, a precious gift indeed.

2 Aids to memory

Most people, however, have a supply of aids to memory; I think of things like address books, with telephone numbers, and Christmas card lists and perhaps a birthday book. A different kind of aid is an album of photographs which remind us of holidays spent, and also perhaps rub in the fact that we used to be younger a few years ago. When one is away from home for any length of time (I think of servicemen) or when our family get married and have moved away, photographs do not so much remind us what they look like but rather help us to keep them in mind. They may be far away in distance, but the photographs to some extent make them present. Other mementoes do the same, even of people who have died; something they gave us keeps their memory alive.

This is one of the many truths about Holy Communion. The words Jesus used at the Last Supper mean 'To remember me, do this'; and he took the bread and broke it and shared it. Whatever other reasons we may have for coming, the chief reason is that Jesus asked us to remember him this way and in a very real way it brings the past into the present. We have the further promise of Jesus that when two or three are gathered together in his name, he is there among them.

3 Remembering the wrong things

No one has an unlimited memory and, while there are some experiences we are unlikely to forget, we can to some extent control what stays in our memory. By thinking again of a person or an experience we revive the memory of them, and the mementoes we have help us to do this. But if our memory and our character are the two things we take with us into the next world, it is all the more essential that our memories should be filled with the right things. Some people manage to keep a grudge alive for years, perhaps keeping letters about it in a secret place known only to themselves; they nurse the memory of unkindness and in its turn it poisons their own mind. In addition to a memory we need a good 'forgettery', into which we can put those things which ought to be forgotten.

4 Aids to forgetting

The secret of forgetting is to fill our minds so full of other thoughts that the experience we want to forget does not get a chance to be remembered. It is rather like making a new recording on a casette; what was there before gets erased. Think again and again of kindnesses done by others, and of the many blessings of God, and your memory will be worth much. St Paul puts it so simply. 'Whatsoever things are true, honest, just, pure, lovely and of good report . . . think on these things.' These things will drive out the things that ought to be forgotten. In this lies the secret of forgiveness. People who say, 'I forgive you, but I will never forget', have not really forgiven. God's forgiveness of us is so happily expressed in the phrase, 'Their sin will I remember no more.' If from the bottom of our heart we can say, 'For your sake, I wish I had not done this or that,' God treats us as though it had never happened.

ST MATTHIAS (14 MAY)

John 15.16 (AV) *'You have not chosen me, but I have chosen you.'*

1 Christ's choice

It was to be expected that by some means a replacement should be found for Judas Iscariot, who had betrayed his master and killed himself. The reading from the Acts of the Apostles gives us the account of his selection. The qualification of the new twelfth man should be that he was one of those who had been with the remaining eleven since the start of the public ministry of our Lord, and had been a witness with them of the resurrection and of the ascension. Two names were proposed. We have never heard anything of either of them before, and we never hear anything about either of them again. Whatever the method of drawing lots involved, the prayer of Peter, 'Lord, you know the thoughts of everyone, so show us which of these two you have chosen as an apostle in the place of Judas', makes it clear that the decision was to be Christ's choice, not theirs.

2 Without distinction

Considering how little we know about Matthias, it makes one wonder why we (and thousands and thousands of other parishes all over the world) should commemorate him every year with a special holy day. If he had been a martyr, or a great missionary preacher, or had founded a church in some far-off city, we could understand. Perhaps if there had been all the means of publicity then that we have now, we should have more reason to remember him. But that could apply to many others, including some of the twelve disciples; even if we could remember all their names, we should have to give up if we were asked for any further information about Thaddaeus. On the other hand, perhaps the very fact that we know nothing more about Matthias is significant. Sanctity and human achievement or distinction are two quite different things.

3 The unknown faithful

Matthias stands as an example of those men described in the Apocrypha 'which have no memorial . . . but these were merciful men, whose righteousness hath not been forgotten . . . Their bodies are buried in peace, but their name liveth for evermore.' (Ecclus. 44.9–14). The world is full of them, thank God, though we tend to take them for granted. Perhaps their supreme quality is that of faithfulness. In any profession or calling, there will be some who get to the top and are given extra responsibiity as a consequence; inevitably they become well known at the time. If the profession has certain standards expected of it by the outside world, there may be those who fail to meet those standards. These are also likely to be well known at the time. In between those two small groups will be a large .

body of faithful people, giving good service and living peaceably. When you are ill and have to be taken to hospital you take it for granted that a nurse – and lots of other people – will be there. There are all the societies which care for the aged, the handicapped or for orphan children; we may send them an annual subscription, and then forget about them till next year. Meanwhile they get on with their job faithfully. There is a happy epitaph in Bemerton Church to a former vicar called Francis Warre, it reads, 'He loved the flowers of his garden, the stones of this church and the people of this parish.' The pace of life may be different today, but the faithfulness expected is the same.

4 An appeal for thanksgiving

There is an ancient legend that God has ordained that at any time there shall be on the earth thirty-six saints, whose identity is known only to God himself. As each dies, so his place is taken by another, whom God has prepared. Of course this is only a legend, but the point is true. Thank God for those many people who have unknowingly helped you on your Christian pilgrimage. As we thank God for his choice of Matthias, the disciple of whom no more is known, so we thank him for all who have no memorial but who served their master faithfully.

ST JOHN THE BAPTIST (24 JUNE)

> Luke 3.15–16 (AV) '*As the people were in expectation, and all men mused in their hearts of John, whether he were the Christ, or not; John answered, saying unto them all, "I indeed baptize you with water; but one mightier than I cometh . . ."*'

1 John's harsh style

It is difficult for us who live after the event, and have the whole gospel story available, to imagine that anyone could wonder whether John the Baptist were the Christ or not. Perhaps I am timid, but John's preaching would have frightened me out of my wits. It sounds like blood and thunder, similar to the hell-fire type of sermon that one associates with those ultra-evangelical preachers of last century. Perhaps there have been so many movements warning us of the end of the world that we no longer take the idea seriously. (In fact, with nuclear bombs, the sudden end of the human race is a greater possibility now than at any previous time in history).

2 John different from Jesus

The contrast between Jesus and John, both in preaching and life-style, seems immense. John lived rough, a definite ascetic. 'John came neither eating nor drinking, and they say, He hath a devil. The Son of man came eating and drinking, and they say, Behold a gluttonous man, and a winebibber, a friend of publicans and sinners.' (Matt. 11.18–19). John warned men to flee from the wrath to come; it sounds like a message of fear. Jesus appealed to men to enter into life; his was a gospel of love. Even the preaching of John about the coming of the Christ sounds like a warning. 'He will throughly purge his floor, and gather his wheat into the garner; but he will burn up the chaff with unquenchable fire' (Matt. 3.12). It is only too easy to contrast the severity of all this with the gentleness of Jesus, and the homeliness of his parables, by which children are introduced to the Christian message. We have to admire the courage of John the Baptist, and we know that he met his end in prison because he had openly rebuked Herod on account of his matrimonial affairs.

3 John and Jesus not contradictory

But is the contrast as clear as all this? Was the teaching of Jesus all that different? When Herod heard about the teaching and the miracles of Jesus, he said, 'It is John, whom I beheaded; he is risen from the dead.' No doubt Herod's conscience was not at rest, but if the contrast had been all that great he would scarcely have said that. Jesus acknowledged that John was his forerunner and it might be expected that he would link his early teaching with what John had been saying. There are, indeed, several such instances, some of which are quite striking. When the Pharisees and Sadducees came to John, he exclaimed, 'O generation of vipers, who hath warned you to flee from the wrath to come? Bring forth therefore fruits meet for repentance' (Matt. 3.7–8). In part of the teaching of Jesus (Matt. 12.31–37) almost identical words are used. The imagery of good trees bearing good fruit, and corrupt trees that will be cut down, is exactly the same. The teaching about the end of all things and the certainty of judgement is very similar.

Jesus did start his teaching from where John had to leave off. He acknowledged openly that John had been his forerunner, preparing the way for him. He took up the theme of judgement, and the need for a revolution in morality. What John could not have foreseen was that Jesus would be initiating a new order and not just bringing an old order to an end. For Jesus, the kingdom of God was not only to be expected, but welcomed and prayed for. To enter into it would require as much change of heart as the judgement which was the theme of

101

the preaching of John. In a sense John is giving a warning, and Jesus promising a new life. What is common to both messages is the need for repentance, for a change of heart and outlook and of one's way of life.

4 The essential message of repentance

The preaching of repentance remains an essential part of the Christian message. It is common to both Old and New Testament. 'Rend your heart, and not your garments, and turn unto the Lord your God' (Joel 2.13) may seem very much an Old Testament theme. But at the close of the great sermon by Peter at Pentecost, those who heard it said, 'Men and brethren, what shall we do?', to which the reply comes at once 'Repent and be baptized.' There can be no acceptance of the salvation Jesus came to bring without repentance. John the Baptist was indeed preparing the way for Jesus. His message of repentance remains essential as a preparation for the coming of Christ into our hearts.

ST JAMES THE APOSTLE (25 JULY)

Mark 10.35–37 (AV) *'James and John, the sons of Zebedee, came unto Jesus, saying, "Master, we would that thou shouldest do for us whatsoever we desire." And he said to them, "What would ye that I should do for you?" They said unto him, "Grant unto us that we may sit, one on thy right hand, and the other on thy left hand, in thy glory."'*

This request by James and John was very understandable. They had given up the family business to become members of this new movement, then there should be some reward; after all, they were just about foundation members.

102

1 Unconditional discipleship

Our Lord's reply is two-fold. First a direct question as to whether their response to his call was whole-hearted; would they keep going and share with him, whatever the cost? They say they are prepared for that. He then says that it is not for him to promise a reward. Following Jesus must be unconditional; for better, for worse – for richer, for poorer. It is not a contract which can be cancelled if either side does not keep certain conditions.

Jacob, when he had his dream in the desert, tried to make such a contract with God. 'If God will be with me, and will keep me in this way that I go, and will give me bread to eat, and raiment to put on, so that I come again to my father's house in peace; then shall the Lord be my God: and this stone, which I have set for a pillar, shall be God's house; and of all that thou shalt give me I will surely give the tenth unto thee' (Gen. 28.20–22).

Following Christ, or more correctly going through life with him, is not like that. James and John said they were prepared to stay with Jesus and share his lot, whether good or bad. As the gospel story develops, we see how closely these two disciples, together with Peter, did share with Jesus. On many occasions, not least at the transfiguration, Peter, James and John were chosen to be particularly close to Jesus. Their conscience must have been all the more troubled at having deserted their master when he was arrested. Later, however, in the strength of the risen Christ they witnessed for him and were ready to suffer. As we know from the biblical record (Acts 12.2) James suffered martyrdom because he was a Christian.

2 An understudy of Christ

Many years ago, at Oberammergau, I wondered what arrangements were made for an understudy to take over if the actor playing the part of Christ were to be ill. The reply to my enquiry was very enlightening. Of course there was an understudy and, unless he was needed to take over the part of Christ, he played the part of James. James, I was reminded, had very little to say and very little to do, but he was close to Jesus throughout the whole play and so was able to watch his action and movements and copy them at a moment's notice if required. I do not know if this happens at every Passion Play, but what a privilege it suggests—chosen to be the understudy of Christ.

This is the calling of every Christian, to be Christ's understudy in the world today. When his word needs to be spoken, we are called to speak it; when his hand would be stretched out, we are called to stretch out ours on his behalf. The qualification is the same as that of St James, namely, that we spend our time close to Jesus, hearing his word and watching his actions. Our Christian life, our times of prayer and Bible-reading and our times of worship, especially of Holy Communion, are all directed to this one end – to be close to Jesus. 'Where I am, there shall my servant be'; this is both our calling and our reward. We are called to be with him hearing his word, but maybe also sharing suffering. The penitent thief who from an earthly point of view shared suffering with Jesus more closely than anyone else was given a very personal promise, 'Today thou shalt be with me in paradise.'

3 Proximity to Christ is the reward

The mother of James and John asked that their reward might be to be next to him, one on each side, in his kingdom. That, in fact, is the reward—the final end of discipleship. Jesus calls us to be close to him, in vision (seeing the world as he sees it), in service, in suffering, in strength and in eternity. Our willingness to be close to him is a measure of our love; equally the joy that results is in proportion to our love.

DEDICATION FESTIVAL

Genesis 28.17 (AV) *'Jacob said, "How dreadful is this place! This is none other but the house of God, and this is the gate of heaven."'*

1 Jacob's assurance of God's presence

On a Dedication Festival, these words come naturally to mind. This church building is for us the house of God and the gate of heaven. But let us think about the background of the text. Esau had a violent grudge against Jacob and was threatening to kill him. Their mother arranged for Jacob to leave home, and sent him to her brother Laban's home. This involved a journey through very uninviting country, a land of prickly pears and scorpions. Far worse however was being away from home and family and, as he would have believed, from the God of his home and family. As far as he was concerned, it was a God-forsaken place. In his dream he learned that it was far from God-forsaken. The ladder of his dream linked earth and heaven; they touched, for him, at the very point where he had been.

2 Assurances for us
   (i) A Church

Of course the presence of God is not restricted to certain holy places; we know that. God is as present in our homes and in our place of work as he is in a consecrated church building: he is as much with us and as near to us on weekdays as on Sundays. But it remains true that there are certain moments in life when we have been more aware of the presence of God than at other times. Probably there have been a few occasions, too precious to talk about, when we were particularly aware of God's presence; then, for us, heaven and earth touched. Equally this church building, set apart from all secular and profane use, is

105

both a reminder and an assurance of the presence of God. In a church building, we are encouraged to open our eyes to perceive something more than meets the eye.

(ii) Significant events

Think of those turning points of family life, when we come to church for some special personal event. For example at a wedding, which is a very earthly event embodying an agreement by a man and a woman to live together and bring up a family, the parties concerned are encouraged to see it as something much more. For the bridegroom, the bride is more than a pretty girl; she is the embodiment of unconditional love, the gift of God to support him all through life. At the moment when the priest declares that God has joined them together heaven and earth touch for them. Again, at the baptism of their children, they are encouraged to realise that they are children of God – entrusted to them to care for, to nurture and bring up. Perhaps at a funeral it is easier to feel the touching of heaven and earth, when this life and the unseen life beyond merge into one another. Of course this experience is not felt every time, nor with equal vividness when it is felt at all.

(iii) Regular worship

Then there is the regular worship which goes on here week by week. Of course, God is not any more present when the bell stops ringing and the service begins. On the other hand, in varying degrees we try to concentrate on offering our worship and hearing the record of God's activity in Christ. In Christ heaven and earth touched all the time; in our worship, earth and heaven seek to touch as we 'our hearts to heaven and voices raise.' In Holy Communion, in particular, something that is very earthly – bread and wine – becomes the occasion for heaven and earth to touch. In a mystery beyond our understanding, the life that was given for us is given to us. By no means do we feel anything supernatural every time, but we know in our heart of hearts that *Holy* Communion means what it says.

3 God's universal presence

Yes, this church building is like the foot of Jacob's ladder, where our prayers ascend and the grace of God comes down to us; and the Lord stands above it all and assures us of his blessing. Indeed, the more we realize his presence here the more readily we shall realize his presence in our homes and everywhere else.

Other Mowbray Sermon Outlines

Series Editor: D. W. Cleverley Ford

Preaching through the Christian Year
Vol. 7 by Alan Dunstan
Vol. 8 by Frank Colquhoun

Preaching at the Parish Communion
Series 3 Service and Lectionary
Vol. 4 Gospels (Year One) by Hugh Fearn
Vol. 5 Gospels (Year Two) by Hugh Fearn
Vol. 6 Gospels, Epistles, Collects (Year One)
by Frank Colquhoun
Vol. 7 Gospels, Epistles, Collects (Year Two)
by D. W. Cleverley Ford

Preaching on Special Occasions Volume Two
by D. W. Cleverley Ford

More Preaching from the New Testament
by D. W. Cleverley Ford

Preaching through the Acts of the Apostles
by D. W. Cleverley Ford

Preaching at the Parish Communion ASB Lectionary
Gospels-Sundays: Year One by Dennis Runcorn
Gospels-Sundays: Year Two by Raymond Wilkinson